The Conscious Sensuality Empowerment

The Conscious Sensuality Appr

Table of Contents

Foreword

Chapter 1: Introduction to Conscious Sensuality
Why this work is important to me
What is Conscious Sensuality
Conscious Sensuality and Tantra: Exploring the differences
Conscious Sensuality as Planetary Healing
Doing Sexual Healing Work
Changing yourself Rather than the World
The Difference between Discernment and Judgment
The Intersection of Mutual Desire
Cleaning your Attic and your Basement
Letting go of the Fear of Intimacy
Acknowledging our Fears
The Desire for Connection
Total Sexual Freedom

Chapter 2: The SET Approach to Sensation, Emotion and Thought
Emotional Abandonment
Gaining Emotional Strength
What is Addiction?
The difference between Feelings and Emotions
The Importance of being Concise and Precise
The Importance of Tone
Are you Communicating for Connection or Release?
Increase Attention Rather than Stimulation
Having a Personal SET Daily Practice
Ideologies are Seductive

Chapter 3: The 3 Step Communication Model
The Conscious Emotional Release Practice
The Reasons for Non-Verbal Emotional Release
The Witnessing Circle
ZEGG Forum
Communicating for Connection
Entering the Spotlight
The Practice of Revelations
The Practice of Feedback
Judging and Being Vulnerable
Embracing the Shadow

Discerning with Whom to Develop Intimacy
Communicating for Decision-Making
Plausible Deniability
Why we say "Yes" when we mean "No"

Chapter 4: The Role of Touch
The Elbow to Fingertip Practice
Expanding the Range of Sensation
Levels of Physical Intimacy: Finding your Edge
Expanding the Range of Sensation and Emotion: Touch Rituals
-Power Spots
-Airbrushing
-Anointing Whole Body
-Chest/Heart/Breast
-Pelvic Release
-Genital
Painful and legal or Pleasurable and illegal?
Hand and Body Positions for Genital Touch Sessions
Exterior Yoni Massage
Connecting with the Clitoris
Pulsing the Introitus
Reframing Penetration as Envelopment
The Clock Exercise
De-armoring the Cervix
Reclaiming the G-spot
Activation and Expansion
The 3 Main Aspects in Genital Touch
To orgasm or not
The Importance of Meditation and Eye-gazing
Resistance
Zen Sex and going slow
Re-Patterning Masturbation as Self-Pleasure
Anal and Prostate Pleasure
The Self-Pleasure Ritual
Hygiene, Safety and Ethics

Chapter 5: Giving Sexual Healing and Empowerment Sessions
Integrity and Staying Grounded
Empowerment and Deep Listening
Entering the Agreement Field
When to Focus on the G-spot
Consent and Informed Consent
Developing a Personal Ethical Framework
Disconnection and Dissociation
What would a Sex-Positive Culture Look Like?
Approaching a Sexual Healing and Empowerment Session

Talk Therapy only goes so far
How can you find a Sexual Healer?
The Intake Form
Clearing the Emotional Field before Touch
Moving beyond reflective "No's" and Inauthentic "Yes's"
Dropping into Deeper Levels of Touch
Ethics Regarding Intimate Touch
Sex Magic and Shamanism
Towards an Erotic Ethics Forum
The Basic Sequence of a Conscious Sensuality Sexual Healing and Empowerment Session
Re-patterning Sexuality From a Sympathetic to a Parasympathetic Response

Chapter 6: Community and Conscious Sensuality
From Political Activist to Cultural Activist
Sense of Community
Collectivist and Communitarian Groups
Masculine and Feminine Aspects of Leadership
The Role of Community in Supporting Erotic Relationships
Non-Rational Practices: Dancing and Dreaming
When Men Do Not Dance
Dreaming a New Culture

Foreword

I work in the field of conscious sensuality because it is a powerful means to bring more health and joy and into people's lives. The more we are satisfied and joyful in our relationships with ourselves and one another the less we are tempted to meet our needs by addictive, unconscious behaviors that deplete our natural energy, joy and enthusiasm for life.

When we are perfectly comfortable revealing our emotional and intimate selves to a larger group of people, we are capable of living more closely with them, i.e. tribally, which is what we need to do to regenerate our environment. People are lonely, but the fears associated with living closely with others, combined with legal and financial challenges to community living keeps people apart. When we trust ourselves to share our truth no matter what, and when we are more excited than scared by the prospect of greater intimacy and connection, then we can move into a lifestyle that is fulfilling and more ecologically sustainable.

Everyone has heard the saying that a chain is only as strong as the weakest link. For many people, that link is sensuality and sexuality. This is where people collapse emotionally and relationships and communities fall apart. Often we have such unmet needs and so little experience in getting those needs met that it takes very little to trigger people into emotions of great desperation and fear.

The less fear we have in communicating the truth of our experiences, the less emotional charge we put into the space and the easier it is for someone to hear. I am more interested in building intimate connection and trust than I am in maintaining a sexual relationship. I have enough experience with friends and lovers, and with former lover who have remained friends, that I do not feel any scarcity around love, sex and intimacy.

I know that as long as I keep myself honest, clearly communicate with others, and release whatever emotions emerge; I will have an abundance of connection in my life. If I become attached to the idea of someone remaining a sexual partner, I would be more likely to hide parts of myself, reducing intimacy in the hopes of preserving our sexual connection. This is a fool's bargain, for no healthy sexual relationship can exist in the absence of intimacy and honesty.

We do not need to spend so much time stimulating our sexual energy or on tactics to build sexual excitement with a lover. Instead we can focus on generating our own natural energy through yoga, meditation, nourishing food, sleep and release of emotional charges so we can stay present in the moment and feel the truth of our connection and desire with another person.

Sexual connection is the fruit of health, joy and connection to oneself, not a strategy to cope with loneliness, fears of inadequacy, or emotional release through cathartic orgasms.

It is not that one should refrain from sex if he/she does not feel incredibly vibrant and full of self-love. It is simply important to notice self-talk about reasons for sexual connections or lack thereof. In short, rather than focusing on how to get someone to be sexually interested in you, the best path to attracting interest from others is to nourish oneself.

Before adding a bunch of tantric, Taoist or esoteric teachings to our sex lives, we do well to take a few preliminary steps: 1) make an accurate assessment of what we want, 2) identify why we want it (is it a goal or a strategy?), and 3) release all that is in the way of receiving love and connection.

This is scary. To be honest with others requires we be honest with ourselves and, in the process, risking appearing less attractive to others. In essence, we need to clean house before filling ourselves up with someone else's concepts and techniques. Once the space is empty, let us not rush to fill it up, but rather selectively integrate what resonates at a deep level and learn to be at peace with not having all the answers.

We do not need to have a completely integrated psycho-spiritual-sexual intellectual framework to have connection and love in our lives, just honesty, curiosity and courage.

CHAPTER 1:
Introduction to Conscious Sensuality

My History

I sometimes find it hard to believe that I am living this life. I grew up in a middle class, suburb of Washington DC. I played sports, loved nature, and loved going the beach with my family. I was interested in history and government. When I realized my young boys dream of being a professional athlete was not to be, my interest politics deepened. I read newspapers, books, and participated in discussions with my family about the daily news.

I was born in 1967 when the Vietnam War was raging. My Dad made several trips to Vietnam and Southeast Asia during the war as a lawyer for the State Department and Pentagon. Even so, my mother argued against the war and wrote letters in opposition to congressmen and senators. She also was an ardent feminist who put an "ERA Now!" bumper sticker on the family station wagon.

My mother had dreamed of being a lawyer as well, but not many women were lawyers when she graduated from the University of Wisconsin in the 1950's. For me, her life has come to symbolize the pain of not following one's dreams. As time went by, she became more depressed and cynical. While loving to her children, she was very resentful toward my father. She would verbally emasculate him in front of my sister and I on a daily basis. Dinnertime was a nightly episode of my mother skewering my father.

Why didn't she just leave if she was so unhappy in her life and relationship with Dad? Why did she sit and stew in a toxic soup of anger, depression and unlived dreams? I think it was because she did not want to break up the family. It was the 1970s, divorce rates were escalating, and many families were enduring the pain of marital breakup, but my mother chose to put her needs aside and defer her own desires.

I remember trying many times to console my mother when she was in "one of her moods." I think this is why I became highly sensitive, empathic, and attuned to emotions, especially with women. Of course, I did not have any tools to work with beyond my love for my mother and desire to see her happy.

If I were to psychoanalyze the situation, I would say I became a substitute for my dad in the realm of intimacy with my mom. I took on her pain, and was often sick as a child. It was an unconscious bargain; I would take care of my mother's emotions to soothe her, and she would take care of me when I was sick. Of course now I see that I might not have been sick nearly as often with bronchitis, the flu, asthma and respiratory illnesses if I had known how to release my emotions, especially the ones I absorbed from my mother. Additionally, Mother's two packs a day cigarette habit did not help my respiratory health.

I wonder if she ever considered that her smoking affected my asthma. She even smoked in the car while driving me to yet another doctor appointment. For years, I was given allergy shots once or twice a week. Even as an adult, and as I became a pot smoker, I would almost always have sinus congestion. I believe this congestion was very much related to emotional stagnation that would manifest as a runny nose. In re-evaluation counseling, the language of an unconscious, only partially expressed emotion is a *leaky discharge*.

When people are afraid to experience and express their emotions, the result is often leaky discharge. And people will manifest physical symptoms that give them permission to discharge. Since my wife and I separated and I prioritized my needs, desires and emotional health, I rarely have been sick. And when I am, it is usually tied to stress and unexpressed emotions. In this process of development, I traded in marijuana for a daily yoga practice.

I have become highly sensitive to my own emotions, and I can now express and release them without damaging others or myself. I am clear about my emotions most of the time and aware that I can be reactive when someone else tells me what my emotions are.

I have come to realize how important it is for me—and I believe for everyone—to feel safe in experiencing and expressing their emotions and desires. While I did not grow up in a religious family with severe limitations around sensual expression, I did grow up in a fairly emotionally repressed environment. My mother's frequent tirades directed at my Dad were not conscious responses but reactive discharges enabled by the loosening effects of alcohol.

My Dad was a participant in this dynamic. He tended to be very quiet and read his newspapers, congressional records, work memos or watch TV. As far as I could tell he engaged with my mother very little. Unfortunately my mother's frustration and anger pushed him even further into his own world, cut off from her and the rest of the family.

This is why we must release our own emotions in a safe way so we can be available to understand and connect with others. Rather than shaming, blaming and giving "shoulds" to others, we can acknowledge what emotions we experience and what we want.

This is why it is so important to have counselors, coaches or therapists who will not absorb our emotions or stories about others, and who will not argue or block the release of our emotions. My mother needed attention to release her emotions, and yet the more she shamed, blamed and screamed, the less inclined my father was to relate with her at all. I imagine he did not feel safe to express his own emotions and would keep them bottled up until he would explode and shout, "fuck you" and leave the room, which happened once or twice a year

I am sure my father wanted love, connection and support like everyone else. And as a man who worked in fairly high levels of government, he had little opportunity to receive emotional support.

All this is not to say that I had a terrible childhood with awful parents who ruined my life. I did experience joy as a kid, particularly when I was playing sports or at the beach. We had an oceanfront vacation home in North Carolina where we would go several times a year. Breathing fresh air, swimming in the ocean and seeing my parents happy always made for the best vacations. And, being in nature was my sanctuary.

Why This Work is Important to Me

When I think about people who are able to give love unconditionally, I imagine they are living in the present moment and not burdened by past hurts or unexpressed emotions. This allows them to see others with an open mind and heart, and receive emotions in a way that opens the mind and heart of others as well. They not are perfect or morally superior; they just have more space to allow others into their lives.

To open up this space, however, we must learn how to release our emotions and judgments in a way that serves those around us and ourselves. This key skill is often lost on people when they are grasping for better relationships and healthy emotional states. Just expressing our emotions is not enough. To truly release emotions we need a process that enables release to occur. Screaming at someone (or worse) may express an emotion, but will not *release* it. Releasing the emotion requires *empathy*, which can be felt with a friend, a counselor, or alone if necessary. Ultimately, it is essential that we learn how to give ourselves empathy and clear our emotional body, but this is an advanced practice. In the beginning of the journey, it is crucial to seek out empathy from others in order to learn the processes and break through your wall of fear, shame, and self-judgment.

Emotional healing is the fundamental work of a sexual healer. When working in the realm of sexuality, we can easily shut down or blow out because the emotions are so intense and the sensations so acute. Shutting down or blowing out happens when we have emotions that exceed our ability to assimilate and express them with consciousness. If we want to move past emotional numbness and reactivity that pushes others away, we do well to increase our emotional range and our awareness about what exactly we are experiencing.

Our task is to first work on ourselves to get to know our inner terrain, which means to understand our learned, conditioned reactions to different types of stimulation. It means learning what we like and what we dislike, distinguishing between our desires and our addictions, loving ourselves even when we are very disappointed, and loving others even when we do not understand them.

Early in life, most of us are taught to do things we do not want to do. Interestingly, *how* we are encouraged to learn or do new things can make a huge difference in who we become. If we are compelled by fear, threats, or intimidation, we may become passive victims or resist and rebel. If we are bribed with sweet rewards, we may become narcissistic and self-absorbed with a tendency to evaluate everything in terms of how it impacts us. If we are given understanding, love, empathy, and supported in our inherent freedom, we will develop self-confidence and the ability to give understanding, love and empathy to others.

It is not too late. Even those with tragic, traumatic childhoods can experience understanding, love, and empathy, and begin to fill their drained emotional reservoirs so they may be fulfilled and give to others. The more we receive, the more we are able to give. Unfortunately, many people have been so conditioned by fear through threats, intimidation and manipulation that their fears feel normal. And these fears are magnified when it comes to sexuality.

When there is trauma associated with a particular part of the body, it gets stored there emotionally. And when we touch that part of our bodies, or even think of it being touched, we can be transported back to that time in our lives when the trauma occurred. The fear, confusion, sadness and frustration many people experience sexually as adults is directly related to the emotions we experienced as children when we discovered the pleasurable sensations of our bodies, including our genitals.

Think about it, why should we discourage children from pleasuring themselves? Genitals are one of the most sensitive and pleasurable areas of the body. Touching our genitals in a pleasurable manner communicates self-love. Most children learn to hide their self-pleasuring activities out of fear due to the shaming of parents and others. This shows up in adulthood as a fear of touching ourselves in the presence of a lover. Overcoming this fear is a fundamental step toward sexual liberation and self-love.

What is Conscious Sensuality?

Conscious Sensuality is the practice of become more conscious by utilizing and expanding on the information we receive through our senses. It is not focused just on sexuality. But sexuality is a key aspect of Conscious Sensuality because in sexuality we experience some of the most intense sensations and emotions in our lives. By exploring our sexuality consciously we are practicing the art of using pleasure for the purpose of greater understanding, compassion, empathy and love.

Conscious Sensuality is a body of work I have developed over many years of working as a sexual healer, massage therapist, counselor, and community leader. It is the way I have learned to navigate my relationships, my emotions, and my sexuality. It is not a rigid ideology or a static school with rules, rather an *approach* to emotions, relationships, and sexuality.

This is crucial because to develop our consciousness we must place primary emphasis on awareness of our own sensations and emotions rather than simply adopting a new ideology whether that be Roman Catholicism, Buddhism, Polyamory, or Tantra. Ideologies are a substitute for sensing, for deeply feeling and a short-cut around critical thinking that integrates our experiences, our emotions and our self-knowledge. Just as a conservative person reads conservative newspapers and a political liberal looks for liberal media, we often unconsciously seek out ideologies that support our unconscious beliefs and patterns of behavior.

When the range of our emotions and sensory experience are limited, we will often substitute thought for emotion and sensation. When we are too caught up in our minds, our lives are out of balance and we are unhealthy. Particularly people who identify with their minds and spend most of their days in front of a computer can be out of balance in regard to sensation, emotion and thought.

This is where we begin our journey into conscious sensuality. We are reprioritizing the value of sensations and emotions in our lives. We are affirming the value of experiencing and expressing those sensations and emotions to the world around us.

The journey into conscious sensuality is one that will help you feel more connected to your body, or "embodied." It will also help you experience emotions more deeply and increase your capacity to *choose* how to respond to emotions. This is a crucial distinction, because just having strong emotions and strong reactions does not indicate a balanced emotional body any more than someone who is unaware and represses their emotions.

Conscious Sensuality & Tantra: Exploring the Differences

When I tell people I work in the field of conscious sensuality I often get a response such as, "Oh, that's like Tantra, right?" I consider Tantra to be one school or approach that is included within conscious sensuality and sacred sexuality. Tantra has its roots in India, and branched out from the culture that birthed Hinduism and Buddhism. It is inextricably linked to religion and exotic to Westerners, and therefore appealing to a certain segment of our culture that is looking for an approach to sexuality not found in the West.

As wonderful as tantric practices and rituals may be, the exotic aspect can distract westerners from the essence of tantra: using sexuality for greater awareness. People can get so consumed in the language, ritual and art of tantra, that they forget it was designed to break the mind free of attachment. They can substitute Tantra for Catholicism, Mormonism or Judaism.

Tantra is like an exotic spice mixture that can make a boring dish more flavorful. Its blend of flavors encourages one to savor the experience of sex. It opens people up to new possibilities. Of course, the term Tantra has been appropriated by people in the west for several decades now and is really a unique, albeit related, approach that evolved from, but is distinct from ancient Tantra. For one thing, neo-Tantra, i.e.: modern westernized Tantra, is much more focused on sex. This has caused many to dismiss neo-Tantra as inauthentic. While neo-Tantra is not Tantra, people in the West use the term because there is no term in English that captures the concept of using sex for greater consciousness.

The pagan west certainly employed sexuality and fertility rituals in the pre-Christian pagan culture. But the stigma attached to the word limits the number of people who may follow teachings called "pagan." While a reverence for sex certainly exists in nature-based religions, nowhere did the use of sex for spiritual purposes reach a flowering as great as in the east.

In China, the concept of Tantra was unknown. Many secret sexual practices were developed and taught through the schools of Taoism. Taoism was less a religion and more an esoteric school of health and wisdom. Mantak Chia is today perhaps the most well known teacher and exponent of ancient Taoist practices, particularly in regard to sexuality. Taoist practices are rooted in concepts of life-force energy generation and health maintenance, and less for spiritual purposes than Tantra.

Tantra, Taoism, as well as other approaches can be put in the category of sacred sexuality. Why not call what we are doing sacred sexuality? Because the work we are doing extends beyond sexuality. Sensuality is a larger field that includes sexuality as well as non-sexual sensuality. In fact, expanding our concept of sensuality to include more than sexuality is a key component to expanding sensual pleasure and healing our sexuality. Let me say that again: By expanding our awareness to include non-sexual aspects of sensuality, we expand our sensual pleasure; we expand our ranges of sensation and emotion, and help heal our sexuality.

Most people link sensuality and sexuality so closely in their minds that it prevents their sensual awareness and enjoyment due to their sexual repression. Everything sensual is seen as sexual. While people may confuse the two, sensual refers to all the senses not just physical touch and the activation of sensors on our skin.

Sensual is nothing more than enjoyment of our senses of taste, touch, sight, hearing and smell. It is true that all of the senses can play a part in sexual excitement and sexual connection. Can we enjoy a hug or a back rub that has no sexual energy behind it? Can we hear beautiful music and feel transported to a place of peace and tranquility?

Our senses give us gifts of pleasure and opportunities for greater awareness. Imagine life with no senses at all. We would hardly seem alive. Yet mind would remain. In fact, sensory deprivation is a key practice that can assist consciousness raising experiences. Sitting in meditation is a form of sensory deprivation that allows us to develop mindfulness and a perspective where we are more conscious of the mind. Sitting, silent meditation is a key practice for building awareness and is a crucial aspect of resetting the emotional body.

By intentionally isolating the senses we can increase our capacity for sensual experience. Blocking out one sense often heightens the perception of other senses, which is why the blind often excel at music. Accordingly, in Thailand, massage is a natural profession for the blind.

So, if the senses distract us from knowing the true nature of our mind, and the goal is to go beyond sensory illusion, why become more conscious of sensuality? Why not pursue the path of traditional meditation, allowing the mind to clear of all thoughts, emotions and sensations? If you are drawn towards traditional forms of meditation such as those found in Buddhism, I encourage you to follow your desire. But be aware that in doing so you are following your desire. And your desire will need to be acknowledged no matter whether your path is one of solitary silent meditation or one of elaborate sexual rituals.

Certainly, traditional seated meditation is a very useful path to gaining awareness of self, compassion and equanimity. But what if one is not drawn to that path? In my case, I used to sit for forty-five minutes every day. It was very helpful in developing my ability to perceive myself. I regularly went to a zendo in Washington DC and I learned the benefits of practicing in a group. These days, while I still do seated meditation, I find myself also drawn to active forms of meditation such as my yoga practice. I do not follow a rigid, daily, seated meditation practice. I have opened to trust my inner guidance and follow my desire as my compass in life.

For many of us, and probably most of us, raised in an environment where parents, teachers and employers used methods to compel us to do what *they* wanted us to do, it is very useful to learn how to follow our desires consciously. And not just desires that are unconscious reactions or rebellions against what someone else wants us to do. Standing tall and owning our desires without judgment or shame allows us to experience the essence of desire. And often, once we have truly experienced a desire, and not just our conception of what it could be, we are freed from the desire.

This type of approach to desire is much more useful than repression and trying to live up to "shoulds" (what others think I should do or be). By repressing myself I may build up my self-discipline, which is very valuable, but I may sacrifice my joy, compassion, and connection with others. And that self-discipline may be more a product of fear than a discipline that helps me reach my goals in life. That is not a trade I am willing to make. Especially when I find that I can follow my desires in conscious ways that lead to joy, compassion and greater connection with myself and others.

The other part of Conscious Sensuality is the conscious part. Why do we say *conscious* as opposed to *sacred*? In my mind, the term sacred has been overused and exploited. While I resonate with the term *sacred sexuality* what we are doing is not just about sexuality or having transcendent sexual experiences. And if you are not comfortable with your sexuality, you may be tempted to slap a sacred label on all of it without examining your choices and behaviors.

In this approach to conscious sensuality, we focus on using our senses to bring greater awareness into our lives. A big part of this work is clearing and strengthening the emotional body. And a key to working in the emotional realm is to ground the experience in the sensual, to get people out of their heads and back into their bodies.

By utilizing practices that encourage us to notice and verbalize the sensations we experience, we become calm and grounded. With this perception of the senses, and ability to communicate the perceptions, we gain perspective on what we are experiencing. Then we can more easily *choose* how to respond to different senses.

And by distinguishing senses from emotions, we gain further perspective and power to choose how we respond and act. By distinguishing sensation from emotion we bring attention to the fact that our emotions can cause sensations in our bodies, and vice versa. Have you ever noticed how the sense of smell can remind you of a past experience that then generates an emotion?

As mammals we have the capacity to experience emotions. Areas of the brain remember, store, and generate emotions. These areas of the brain are simply not present for non-mammals. Most mammals are social creatures, designed to function in social settings where emotions are a very useful evolutionary adaptation.

People, by virtue of our cerebral cortex, enjoy the additional benefit of self-awareness and the capacity to witness our thoughts, emotions, and actions. We focus on expanding this capacity for self-awareness in Conscious Sensuality. If you want, you can only use a small part of your brain and your being and have a sex life that is devoid of awareness, even devoid of emotion. You can be a lizard. There is nothing wrong with being a lizard if you are a lizard. But there is so much more to experience as a fully awake human being.

All the practices we do are designed to increase our ability to see ourselves more clearly. And in doing this we gain freedom and greater ability to see others, which generates compassion, understanding, and love.

If I had to choose between a sexuality that is explosive, transcendent and magical and a sexuality that brings more peace, awareness and compassion to the world I would choose the latter. Fortunately, I do not believe we have to choose. But if we focus on the former, we may be distracted from the greater benefits to others and ourselves.

If one is entranced by sexual experiences and hungers for powerful sexual encounters, I encourage them to explore those desires and turn their fantasies into reality. By remaining present and aware, one can reap additional benefits of those experiences. I am certainly not suggesting that we become sexuality meek and practice only mellow sexual connections. I am suggesting that if we are mindful of our sexuality and sensuality, it can bring greater levels of peacefulness and compassion to our lives. This is the goal, not just the strategy.

Conscious Sensuality as Planetary Healing

One of the reasons for developing and teaching conscious sensuality is that this is a powerful way to bring healing to the planet. The more we are satisfied and joyful in our relationships, the less we are tempted to meet our needs by consumerist behavior that isolates us and degrades the planet. For years I worked in the environmental and political realms and even though I was successful in many campaigns, I felt frustrated by the fact that so many people seemed blind to the destructive environmental impact of their choices.

Now I see that people were disconnected from the environment just as they were disconnected from their bodies and senses. We literally need to come to our senses and get out of our heads. We spend too much time thinking and too little time experiencing. When we are required to make decisions and figure things out, we can do so more easily and efficiently if we are of sound mind and body. If our emotional body is healthy, we are much more likely to make choices that are healthy for others, the environment, and ourselves.

Community living is another important part of conscious sensuality. I believe that we are best served by living in a community of people with whom we share love and trust. We do not need to share sex with other people in our community. We can be perfectly monogamous or even celibate if this is our desire, but we are diminished if we only have one other person to connect with emotionally. Monogamy can be greatly supported by a community of people who can help meet everyone's needs for emotional clearing and physical nurturing. However, the fact that people are often attracted to and desire sexual connection with people other than their partner needs to be understood with openness, and without judgment or shame. Acknowledging our attractions can free us from both repression and indulgence. When we acknowledge our truth, we are freer to consciously choose how we will act.

The less fear I have in communicating the truth of my experiences and my reactions, the less emotional charge I put into the space and the easier it is for someone to hear what I have to say. I am more interested in building intimate connections and trust than I am in maintaining a sexual relationship. Let me say that again: "I have an intention to be more focused on building love and friendship than maintaining a sexual connection."

Sometimes I feel sexual; sometimes I do not. I never judge myself for not being as sexual as some people or more sexual than others. At times, I may truly prefer alone time to a marathon lovemaking session. I can enjoy non-sexual, sensual connection as much as the sexual connection if it is my true desire at that moment.

I like to say, "Desire is my compass." Which can sound selfish and even devilish to those who do not have an understand that following our desires can actually benefit others and the world. I believe that if one follows their desires consciously, that the desire will lead to higher states of awareness.

Doing Sexual Healing Work

To do sexual healing work is to create a safe space where we can breathe and relax. One of the biggest mistakes among healers is when they act like surgeons and try to fix a problem for someone else. We can see others and ourselves as victims in need of repair or sympathy, as heroes who help victims that feed their egos, or we can see life as a spiritual journey where every experience is an opportunity for growth and awareness.

Developing our ability to be present is of utmost importance for a healer. Life is what happens in the present moment. How do we develop that ability?

We are constantly given opportunities to be present if we recognize them as such. Rather than retreating into fear, anger, blame, shame and "shoulds," we can expand into our experiences, note our reactions, choose our responses and honor ourselves.

Our sexuality is often like a cave; a deep dark place where we put everything that scares us. It can also be a place of buried treasure or pleasure that can serve to nourish our lives. When we deny ourselves sexual pleasure, we cut ourselves off from the power to create and generate life.

Healing our sexuality means coming into the present moment. It means honoring and valuing ourselves as worthy of receiving pleasure, however we enjoy it.

When we are sexually satisfied:
-Our presence is enjoyable.
-We attract others and what we need in life.
-We do not seek approval from parents, teachers, lovers or bosses.
-We source our own energy.
-We are content with simple things in life that make our bodies and hearts feel good.
-We have love to give others and this feels good.
-Our need to contribute is met.
-We are less likely to have unhappy relationships when we are sexually whole and satisfied.
-We are less likely to be manipulated by others who use our desire for connection to fulfill their own needs.
-We are less likely to give power to those who are unconscious of their needs.

If there is a political aspect of conscious sensuality and healthy sexuality it is this: Sexually free and empowered people are not likely to participate unconsciously in environmental destruction, war or social and economic oppression.

When we are sexually whole:

-We are more sensitive to our environment when we are sensitive to our emotions and to the sensations in our bodies.
- We are more sensitive to life itself and in alignment with protecting and generating more diversity of life.
-We live more intimately with those around us.
-We are more compassionate with others.
-We love ourselves, and we love our bodies including our genitals.
-We know what we want and can ask for it directly.
-We are content at being non-sexual as well.
-We acknowledge our desires without having to act on them.
-We can take joy in other's sexual enjoyment, including our lovers, ex-lovers, friends, parents and children.
-We pleasure ourselves without shame.
-We appreciate differences in sexual orientation and desire without judgment.
-We talk openly, honestly and without shame, about sexuality.

Changing Yourself Rather Than the World

Before I was a political and environmental activist I was greatly influenced by Buddhist thought. I read and meditated a lot. I was struck by the idea that happiness would be easier to attain by working on myself than working to change the world. Of course working on oneself is no easy task. But compared to changing the world, it is a manageable project.

After some years of environmental work, I realized no matter how hard I worked I could not save the world in my lifetime.

My understanding of the immensity of the environmental and political problems of the world led me to focus on creating the positive rather than fighting the negative. Even when we "won" environmental campaigns, the victories were somewhat hollow in that they were often short-lived or partial victories. Plus, for every one we won, we lost ten, one hundred, or one thousand more.

Upon contemplating this, I realized I wanted to create something positive. I had been gardening for years, teaching permaculture and creating environmental landscapes for clients. I realized I needed to have a balance of positive work to offset the emotional drain of trying to stop some environmental damage.

What I did not realize was that I had another option. I could have done my "negative" work in a positive manner. Rather than being fueled by outrage and fear, and using similar emotions to motivate others, I could work on "negative" issues from a positive viewpoint.

Similarly when I work on my own "negative" issues, I try to do so with a positive outlook. This is not just the simplistic approach of "think happy thoughts" or only express positive emotions. Rather, by taking a conscious approach to releasing emotions, we can truly release the negative emotions, which are simply the emotions we are not enjoying. By consciously choosing to release emotions we are acting positively.

I have by no means given up on others or the planet; I just want to be as effective as possible. I find that the best way to serve others is to be conscious of my desires and in alignment with them. For many years I strove to bury my desires and be a "good person" as a way of meeting my needs. But when I acted counter to my desires, my emotional body sabotaged my efforts at connection and fulfillment. I needed to make peace with my desires. If we do not really want something, we are not going to get much benefit out of it and, on a subconscious level, people around us are not going to truly appreciate our efforts. Our inauthenticity will ring false for them and they may tell themselves they should appreciate us, but their emotional body will not experience or fully express appreciation.

On a spiritual level, this approach aligns me with the desires of the universe, nature or God. I thought long ago that if my mind could release my ego and become one with God, I would not experience much of a jolt when my body dies. To become the mind of God is to let go of individual attachment and obsession with this particular body and life.

In my mind, the way to accomplish this is not to deny myself and try to reach some external standard of behavior or morality. Acting as naturally as possible, that is, in accordance with my natural desires, is to merge with Nature and God.

I am not suggesting we blindly follow our desires and become animalistic by relating to instinct alone. This is actually impossible; if we deny our humanness we will be damaging ourselves in the process. When we deny our emotional body, we create illness as a means to get our attention.

In my case, childhood illness suggested I had unexpressed sorrow and inability to communicate my emotions. As an adult, I am rarely ill. The inner work I have done led me to believe that my illnesses were a way of getting attention. My mother's smoking habit was an attempt to stuff or burn her unmet emotional needs.

In the 70s, Smoking was a socially acceptable form of passive suicide. If you had unmet needs and were unable to speak them, you could make an unconscious choice to kill yourself. Sometimes I reflect on the fact that smoking was acceptable back then and that other behaviors are socially acceptable at different times and in different cultures. Why are smoking or overeating acceptable, but group sexual exercises condemned? The closer we get to seeing and feeling our unconscious patterns, the more fear and resistance they generate. When resistance is generated, we may need to make up stories to explain the sensations being experienced in our bodies.

This is why it is so important to talk about "story." For anything that happens, any sensation or emotion we experience, our mind likes to come up with a story to explain or justify it. The process of generating stories may actually keep us unconscious. Re-evaluating or examining our stories is a way to gain freedom and become conscious.

In Hawai'i where I live, people "talk story" with each other. They share the news of the day, how they feel, and they often gossip about others. I like the phrase "talk story," because it reminds me that it's all just a story. I want to "talk story" in as conscious a way as possible so I am not limited by my story. I want to experience my life without being bound to a story.

When we trust we are acting in accordance with Nature or God, we can relax into a space of union. Many people have come to similar ideas and yet it is not that simple. It can be hard to let go of our belief and our ideologies.

Ideologies can separate us from experiencing the truth in our experiences. I define my religious views as, "Experiences not beliefs."

Ideologies can prevent us from deeply seeing others, as opposed to seeing their actions. It is then easy for us to make up stories about why they are doing what they are doing.

It takes more work to be open to people and truly see them instead of judging them as right or wrong. And if I were to say, "Well, people are lazy and they take the easy way out," I would be taking the easy way out by judging them.

Most of us have been strongly conditioned to evaluate everything and everyone as right or wrong, good or bad.

While this is not new information, what I hope is new or useful is the means to evolve beyond this thinking. You can spend a lot of time judging yourself for judging others. Not too much fun!

To follow desires and see where they lead is a powerful tool in raising consciousness and letting go of obsessions, stories, patterns and judgments.

The spiritual teacher Osho told a story about a man who wanted to stop smoking. Rather than giving him a mantra, or medicine or a judgment, Osho told the man to make smoking his meditation and to enjoy it as much as possible.

The man thought Osho was crazy, telling him about all the dangers and health risks of smoking. Yet, his obsession with quitting smoking had not worked. He still smoked and he hated himself for his weakness. In the Hawai'ian conflict resolution process *Ho'o pono pono,* the first step is self-forgiveness.

I am not suggesting that one become a child rapist and murderer if that is your desire. If you have that desire, get professional help to protect yourself and others. But I cannot believe that anyone would be born and naturally develop a desire for raping and murdering. Those desires are the result of other unexpressed, unrealized, and repressed natural desires.

Perhaps politicians who are "tough on crime" and seek punishment for others are projecting their subconscious desires on others. Do laws and punishments really reduce crime? Do you think people who are about to murder someone really stop and think about the consequences of their actions? In my view the most common form of premeditated murder is war. War is the result of unexpressed and unacknowledged emotions by politicians.

So how do we evaluate a desire as natural or not? And isn't that a form a judgment? It does not have to be if we just focus on noticing rather than judging. And if you are judging, you can go into a place of noticing that judgment.

The Difference Between Discernment and Judgment

It is important to distinguish between judgment and discernment. When we judge, we close our eyes and label something good or bad. When we discern, we make a choice for ourselves without universalizing and without making a judgment of what others should do. Discernment requires perceptiveness—both where our needs are concerned and in how we act to fulfill our needs and desires.

The exercises in this book can help you move into a place of noticing more than judging. Try them out and see how you feel. That is the ultimate test of effectiveness.

How do we develop trust in ourselves to make decisions and behave in ways that are beneficial to others and ourselves? Many people are scared to look inside for fear of what would emerge if they truly followed their desire. And many others may complain bitterly that following desire is easy for a single man who is self-employed living in Hawai'i. What about a poor, single mother who works a job she hates to support her family?

That single mom may have fantasies of giving it all up – including her children – and going to live on a beautiful tropical island instead of living and working in Topeka, Kansas. What would prevent everyone from just dropping all their responsibilities and becoming vagabonds and welfare cheats? Or rapists, murderers, and thieves?

The more we cannot conceive of following our desire, the more out of alignment with our desire we are. And often the key to being in tune with our desire is to come into the present moment to actually see what is going on right now, and then make decisions from the present time. So often our decisions or lack of decisions are a reflection of unacknowledged, unreleased, unconscious emotions based on the past or future.

I imagine that the overworked, single mom in Topeka might not make radical changes in her life if she began to follow her desire. If she truly followed her desire, released her emotions and came into the present moment, she would likely stay with her children and forget about moving to that tropical island.

She might get a different job or she might keep her job feeling less emotionally weighed down and more open to creating changes that would benefit her and her children.

As strange as it sounds, I think that my mother would have been better off getting a divorce when I was a kid. No one knows exactly what she was thinking, but looking back, it seems clear to me that she was depressed. She certainly was not empowered to make changes; rather, she complained a lot, mainly about my dad.

Getting a divorce, however, is not necessarily going to increase consciousness, empowerment, and communication skills. Many people get divorced but still, years later, blame their former spouse for "ruining" their lives. They are still married in their minds! By refusing to release emotionally, take responsibility for their lives, and own their desires, they take the weak way out by blaming another person in order to avoid looking at *why* they participated in such a sad story.

The Intersection of Mutual Desire

What emotions come up for you when you think of following your desire? Are you more excited or scared? Can you conceive of desire that is beneficial for you and for others? In conscious sensuality workshops we encourage people to tune into the intersection of mutual desire, that is, the place where your desire intersects with the desire of others. So the game is not just to do what you want to do, but to be in tune with your desire and develop more and more sensitivity and awareness of what others want. Rather than blindly going after what we desire and pushing or manipulating others to give us what we want, we can come from a place of mutual respect, becoming more curious about the desires of someone else. Passively allowing someone to do what they want is not a recipe for building love, trust and awareness.

I am not suggesting to refrain from sex if you lack the feelings of vibrancy and self-love, just notice what you are telling yourself about your reasons for your sexual connections (or lack thereof). Rather than focusing on how to get someone to be sexually interested in you, the best path to attracting interest from others is to nourish yourself. This is why a regular conscious self-pleasuring practice is one of the key practices for generating healthful energy that is attractive to others.

Cleaning your Attic (mind) and your Basement (sexuality)

Just as a friend comes by on a weekend to support you to get rid of the junk you want to get rid and yet are attached to, we help people release and make space for light and air in their bodies, minds and hearts. Our basement is where we store our fear, negativity, body shame, and unexpressed desire. Our attic is where we keep our made-up stories that prevent us from following the truth of our desires.

I remember when I was a boy and my neighbor suddenly died. It was quite a loss for me. No longer would this sweet, calm, grounded older man be part of my life. I also remember how my mother went over every night to sit with the widow. I can still hear my mother's voice saying, "I'm going over to sit with her." Today, I know that by "sit" she meant allow her friend to cry, reminisce, confide, and release. Most importantly, just being present and witnessing the woman was a tremendous help as she dealt with overwhelming emotions. Often, we are afraid to invite someone to witness and hold space for us while we release emotion and come into present time.

When both people in a sexual relationship are in need of emotional release and empathy, they are often not able to get their needs met. It is extremely productive to focus 100% attention on one person at a time so they can release their emotional charges. Unfortunately, without awareness of our need to release emotions, we can get re-stimulated by listening to others as they attempt to release their charges.

A common occurrence is when a woman wants to be witnessed by her man as she releases her emotional charges. The man is uncomfortable and instead gives advice, tunes out, or gets angry.

Until people are skilled at perceiving their own emotional state and needs, communicating and releasing their charges, it is best to do emotional clearing work with someone who is not a sexual partner. I consider it an advanced practice to be able to ground the emotional charges and give empathy to a lover who believes you are to blame for their misery. Give yourself and your lover a break and do regular, conscious emotional release work with others who have an understanding of the importance of this practice and can ground your charges, give you empathy and witness without judging or giving advice.

In re-evaluation counseling (RC) it is advised to seek counseling from those we don't have even a social relationship. Often this is unrealistic, as people who connect through re-evaluation counseling or other modes are likely to have common interests in other areas of their lives.

When I have a strong emotional charge I have a practice of first releasing it with a neutral third party, not a lover. It is not about hiding it from a lover, but releasing the intensity of the charge before sharing it, particularly if it has to do with her. When we release the charge with someone else first, then we can give the information with less charge, which enables us to give it more cleanly, and for the other to receive it more gracefully.

I remember when I first got initiated into re-evaluation counseling I was excited and optimistic about the practice. But my wife voiced fears of sharing details of our life with others. I could not understand this. I reasoned every person and every couple has issues, and ours were not likely to be more extreme or embarrassing than theirs. I think my wife feared that the intimacy generated by the releasing and sharing would result in an affair or desire for sexual connection with someone else. At the time I did lump intimacy and sexuality together so it was a valid concern. But rather than avoiding intimacy with others, a more effective path is to acknowledge the potential of intimacy generating sexual attraction, to be honest about that, and to release it as well.

Letting Go of the Fear of Intimacy

If we are to build healthy lives, relationships and communities, we must let go of our fear of intimacy. Each step we take into honesty and intimacy gives us more strength and courage to step further into the flowing river of the present moment, revealing ourselves nakedly to the world.

The process of cleaning out our attic and basement can be messy. Rarely is it an orderly, aseptic process. If you have a clogged sewer line in your basement, you have a problem. Once the shit starts to flow out, it often comes with a volume and intensity that is related to the strength and duration of the unmet needs. When we are in that space we are needy and less capable of holding space for anyone else. We need help and support from another.

When I was a teenager, each new sexual connection was charged with a potent mixture of excitement and fear. I would often shake, almost to the point of convulsions, when highly aroused.

Many people have intertwined their need for emotional release and sexual connection, and in these cases orgasm becomes a tool for emotional release. This does help to calm the body but can also drain energy and lead to addictive patterns. When we do regular maintenance in sweeping out our attic and basement, our sexuality can take a more natural form. We can connect more with others and ourselves rather than use the experience to release or distract ourselves.

Doing regular self-pleasure practice or practice with another can get us sexually connected and absorb sexual life-force energy even if we don't have a partner or lover. By gaining familiarity with a regular conscious sexual practice, we will not get so distracted by excitement or fear when we do have a mutual sexual connection. And then we can truly see what is actually present between us.

Rather than going to a party after not eating all day and gorging ourselves at the buffet table instead of connecting with guests, let's focus on meeting our needs on a regular basis. From the space of abundance and trust that we can get our needs met, we can be curious to see who shows up and what might happen between us.

To be in the present moment with trust is to be sensitive to our energy and the energy of others. When we are in this position, we naturally attract those to whom we are also attracted.

Acknowledging Our Fears

Another issue that came up for me when I started to open my sexuality was my fear of men. I have always been more comfortable confiding in and developing intimate friendships with women. And since my primary orientation is heterosexual, this meant my need for intimacy was linked with my need for sexual expression.

I did not have many male role models growing up. I was in a suburban nuclear family with few close friends and no extended family. I saw my grandfather and uncles about once a year and we were never close. It never even occurred to me to trust and be honest with them.

I was like my father, who did not have close male friends. He worked in a world of men and yet was far more comfortable with his books than with his colleagues. His high-level work in the military-industrial complex put him in contact with men of an aggressive and violent nature, such as arms traffickers and people involved in the Iran-Contra scandal.

I remember a period of time when he received anonymous death threats over the phone on a regular basis. He was under so much pressure that he had a number of car accidents. I am sure I picked up his anxiety and fear, his lack of trust in other men.

I was always a little unusual as a kid and had difficulty with other boys at school. While I had some friends, I often attracted abusive behavior by the more aggressive boys. Perhaps because of my fear and reactions to their teasing, I was abused more than some others. I remember in fourth grade, as the juice of sexuality started to flow in me and I noticed girls as sexual beings, I'd come home every day, slam my book bag on the floor, and cry in my mother's arms. She told me that the boys were mean to me because I was special. In any case, I developed a fear of men, particularly men who were older or physically stronger than me.

In 9th grade I joined the football team. I was the second fastest boy on the team and had decent skills but no aggressive passion. I remember one game where a kid from the other team ran for a touchdown and I was the only one with a chance of catching him. I caught up with him but could not summon the aggressiveness required to tackle him. He scored the touchdown. I had failed.

My teammates attacked me in the locker room, picked me up, and tried to shove my head into the toilet. I fought back punching one in the face and breaking his glasses. Once I showed aggression they left me alone, perhaps satisfied that I could fight back. For men, displays of aggressiveness create a certain kind of manly trust that we have the strength and the courage to fight and protect each other. Just like in war-training exercises, men practice fighting each other so they can protect each other when a real fight occurs.

This fear of men continued in my life for many years, even when I had a group of male friends in High School and University. I did not join a fraternity because I was turned off by the male bonding or, perhaps more accurately, due to my fear of rejection.

I reckoned with my fear of men when I worked as a door-to-door environmental organizer. Each afternoon I would go out with other organizers and knock on doors to raise money for environmental campaigns. Talking to men, particularly older men, was difficult for me. I assumed a natural familiarity with women but was uneasy around the men.

Overcoming this through practice gave me more confidence and power in my life. My fear of men appeared again when I started to be in intimate and sexual situations where other men were around. The first time I was involved in group sex, I felt completely numb, not the least bit aroused. I was emotionally overloaded and unable to express myself.

This may have been due to the newness of the situation, but later I realized I had a fear of showing my sexual side in front of men. Showing our sexuality is literally physically vulnerable—we are exposing the most sensitive parts of our body. Subconsciously, I was afraid that if I lay down and open to pleasure, a group of men would grab me and abuse me in some way.

Moving past this fear, being open to receiving pleasure in the presence of men has been very empowering. To be receptive is to access our feminine nature. As much as men like to receive pleasure, the fear of being exposed or seen as receptive or feminine keeps many men locked in a barren prison of their own construction. For many men, sex is about getting to *do* something to someone else. Slightly more open is the desire to do something *with* someone else. To be receptive is to *receive* from someone else.

I lived in an experimental sensual community for a time where the men enjoyed giving women pleasure. But most of these same men were resistant to being pleasured by the women. I believe this was due to the fear associated with receiving in front of other men. I think almost all men would be happy to receive if there were no other man present.

There was one man in particular I remember who did not even want to stroke the women and was not open to being pleasured either. He was a strong, physical, alpha male who eventually had sex with almost every woman in the group. Once, just before the start of a practice session, I asked if he going to join us in the practice. He looked panic stricken for a moment, as if to expose his desire to practice and connect would be a sign of weakness. He said no, he was not there to practice, and left.

For some men, even the act of giving pleasure to women is too vulnerable. It suggests issues of power and control as if giving to someone else means being subservient. This is why it is acceptable, even macho for men in some cultures to have sex with other men as long as they are the "top." To be a man and on the "bottom" is to give up manhood. How sad that the idea of receiving pleasure is seen as weak and unmanly. As some would describe it, this is the unhealthy masculine.

I have a friend who is very skilled in the art of giving men anal pleasure. I have had transcendental experiences with her, very ethereal and powerfully energizing. Receiving anally seems to balance out the strong energy in my penis. The more I am grounded through male G-spot or prostate massage, the more capacity for sensation and expansion I have in the rest of my body.

Receiving regular prostate massage is very healthy for the prostate as well. The incidence of prostate cancer is notably less in gay and bisexual men, and notably higher in celibate men such as monks.

The Desire for Connection

If our objective is to feel more connection, love and peace in our lives, then learning to receive as well as give is an important element. Sessions where we are 100% giver or 100% receiver can be very useful in expanding awareness and generating empathy and compassion for others. For many women, intercourse can be painful; for men, rarely so. But for men unaccustomed to anal pleasure, being penetrated can be frightening and painful.

Even our language is biased in favor of the active party, the initiator. This is related to a patriarchal, dominator view of life, society and sex. Just as "bottoms" are disparaged in macho cultures, women are as well. People refer to intercourse from the viewpoint of the initiator, not the receiver. Sometimes I like to refer to intercourse as "envelopment" to turn the tables linguistically. It also implies more pleasure for the initiator than "penetration" suggests. If the penis is being enveloped, it is receiving pleasurable sensations. If the penis is viewed as the penetrator, men's minds may receive an ego-expanding experience such as "I'm getting to fuck this hot girl... look at me." It is not entirely far-fetched to say penetration, in this context, borders on rape. Rape is when one is lost in fantasy and projection, not connecting with self or the other person.

Since I have given myself total sexual freedom, I do not fantasize nearly as much as I did previously. When I have desires or scenes in my mind, I acknowledge them, speak them, and accept that they will either happen or not. So many wonderful things now happen in my life that I do not spend much time fantasizing.

It may seem unfair, but women are very receptive to a man who is sexually free and satisfied. A man who is sexually satisfied is a man who is not driven by hunger and loneliness but by authentic desire for connection. I am not obsessed with "getting inside" every beautiful woman I see, nor do I push for as much as I can "get" when connection is available. Being sexually satisfied, I get a lot of pleasure out of conversation, silent connection, cuddling, massage, and alone time.

Years ago I could not imagine being at a nude beach or hot spring and not being mesmerized by beautiful, naked women. It is important to create a body-positive culture, one that encourages people to feel safe and beautiful being nude outside and socially. By distinguishing nudity from sexuality, we take another step towards a sexual maturity where our pleasure is not tied to some forbidden fruit.

Doing massage work, I am physically intimate and yet non-sexual with many people. Since doing sexological massage and other sex work, I am less distracted by sexual energy during a non-sexual massage. Even if I get turned on during a massage, I can acknowledge that energy and continue the massage without crossing any boundaries, theirs or mine. I have a clear boundary that I will not do any sexological work with anyone unless agreed upon (or left open as a possibility) *before* the session starts.

Women are just as hungry for physical closeness and intimacy as men. Often, it all just gets lumped together with sexuality. Teasing it apart is the work of conscious sensuality. When we can be conscious and at choice about whether to be sexual or not, intimate or not, we have control over our lives and more fulfilling relationships. When we have greater awareness of our different desires such as physical closeness, intimacy and sexuality, we can more successfully integrate them into our lives.

Total Sexual Freedom

Being able to make distinctions between sensations, emotions, and thought enables us to see ourselves, our motives and our desires more clearly.

For the most part, people need to go through a period of total sexual freedom before they can consciously choose to put restrictions on their freedom or to make relationship agreements as to allowed and disallowed activities. Lumping all physical closeness and emotional intimacy together with sexual connections actually threatens monogamy far more than agreements both people truly desire that include the opportunity to be physically close and emotionally intimate with others.

Even if a strict interpretation of monogamy restricts physical closeness and emotional intimacy and successfully maintains sexual exclusivity, a significant percentage of the men are likely to have active fantasy lives full of sexual connections with other women. This seems to me the real tragedy, for when desires are left unexpressed or even just unacknowledged, they can get in the way of being fully present with our partner, as well as with ourselves.

How can we grow strong enough, confident and secure enough in our lives to hear that our partner would like to explore their sexuality with another? If monogamy is tied to our socio-economic status, to our children, and to our need for intimacy and closeness, how likely are we to risk our relationship at the cost of honesty?

Yet without honesty how can there be any true intimacy or connection?

And what about the children? We often hear that a couple stays together "for the sake of the children." Yet what are we teaching children by having them living in the midst of fear, resentment and/or unexpressed desires and fantasies? We are teaching them to suffer. And to lie.

Are we so blind as to not see the connection between living joyfully and pursuing our desires and health? As much as I have eaten what I consider to be a healthy diet for twenty years, it seems clear that joy and being in the present moment is more conducive to health than diet.

You can eat a perfectly organic, raw vegan diet and sabotage your health by obsessing over what you are eating or by judging yourself mercilessly.

Sex and sensuality are a fundamental part of joy. Our sex-negative culture is responsible for so much depression and anxiety. Imagine if we shamed people as much for their food choices as for their sexual choices, branding people who like potato chips as molesters, predators, and spreaders of disease.

By accepting that sexual interest and desire is natural in children, most people would likely move from obsession with sex and physical appearance in their teenage years to a more mature understanding of themselves and relationship by their mid-twenties. It is almost comical to think of trying to teach teenagers math and science in the midst of hormonally-induced obsession that they are required to pretend isn't hijacking their attention throughout class!

Teenagers are biologically programmed to want sexual exploration and connection far more than they want to work on algorithms. This is not to say teenagers should go to school to have orgies everyday. But trying to force them to be celibate and focus on subjects far less exciting than sex is to tell them their bodies and minds are wrong.

Can you imagine a world where teenagers are not given the sterile sex education class but actually given an opportunity to witness and practice loving, sensitive sexuality? Nature abhors a vacuum, and sexually explicit advertising, Internet, movies, magazines, etc., fills the vacuum around sexuality. Rarely is sexuality portrayed in a way that increases consciousness, respect, sensitivity, or health.

When we express our sexuality on a regular basis with a community of people dedicated to awareness, compassion, honesty and self-growth we can experience increased trust, confidence, balance and greater cooperation. When people experience abundance in sensuality and sexuality they are more likely to support and rejoice in others getting their needs and desires fulfilled.

CHAPTER 2:
The SET Approach (Sensation Emotion Thought)

Emotional Abandonment

In Conscious Sensuality workshops we focus on the individual and the whole community, as well as couples. A relationship is only as strong as the people in it. It is so simple, yet people may convince themselves that their partner is to blame for their problems. Even when their partner is long gone they can still serve the function of scapegoat for a less-empowered person.

I remember one holiday dinner at my mother-in-law's house. Over the years it had become a guessing game: whom is she going to pick on during the holiday meal? Sometimes it was me, sometimes it was my wife, or my step-children. But on at least one occasion, the holiday punching bag was her long-deceased husband.

One would have thought the poor guy had just left the dining room table for a moment by the way she spoke. She was so consumed with anger, disgust and judgment it was hard to believe he had died twenty years prior. It was incredible to me that she was so vicious in her attacks, and that we would put up with it.

This was her way of relieving stress after having created the holiday celebration: to judge and ridicule the family around her, all the while espousing her innocence, purity and religiousness. "Never has alcohol touched these lips!" she would say as if auditioning for a part in God's own private army of judgmentalists.

At the time it was annoying, depressing and provoking to be in the midst of such tirades. Of course at that time in my life I enjoyed regular, if less frequent tirades. As I look back I am amazed at how badly I made everyone else out to be in my pursuit of being good.

I was afraid of revealing myself at that time. I preferred to appear good, at least according to my values, if not my mother-in-law's (or my mother's) standards. While I had done a little work with re-evaluation counseling, I had not taken to heart my responsibility for my emotions and for my happiness in life.

I think I was afraid that if I prioritized my happiness I would fail and then where would I be? So I minimized the importance following my desire, instead charting a course as a noble environmental warrior.

Smoking marijuana, even as little as I did, resulted in emotional stagnation and shrinking of my emotional spectrum or range. Smoking marijuana can change one's perspective in some positive ways, but on the whole, it made me *less* aware of my emotions and myself. That was the most deceptive, destructive quality of marijuana for me: the impairment of my emotional body.

I recall a friend remarking that he did not smoke anymore because he valued his "clarity." I wasn't ready to hear it and subconsciously preferring to avoid clarity and being responsible for the choices I was making. In short, I did not have the emotional strength to pursue my desires.

Gaining Emotional Strength?

Some of the most powerful ways we can build emotional strengthen are encapsulated in the SET Approach. In this approach we distinguish Sensation, from Emotion, from Thought. When people speak of their "feelings" they often confuse sensation, emotion and thought, condensing them into something amorphous and ambiguous that becomes evermore difficult to truly feel. With SET, we take a deliberate approach and dissect our experiences into these three aspects of perceptual consciousness.

Sensations, the perception of stimuli, enter us through one of our sense organs: eyes, ears, nose, mouth and skin. Sensations, in and of themselves, are wholly without judgment. They are not mental phenomenon. Hot, cold, dry, wet, loud, aromatic, soft, scratchy, bright, colorful, etc. These are sensations that ground us in the world around us.

What we know of the brain it is clear: it has had at least three major evolutions. The reptilian brain is the base brain, focused on physical survival needs. This is the seat of instinct, sensation and direct response. This brain acts without reference to emotions or self-awareness.

The next major evolution of the brain is the limbic system, which enabled the development of emotions. Emotions are highly complex. Researchers have argued for decades about whether emotions arise from sensations or from thoughts. Do we experience a sensation that leads to an emotion or do we have a thought that leads to an emotion? It is probably not as simple as either.

What is clear is that emotions are a product of the limbic system, which developed in mammals and is absent in most reptiles. The limbic system enabled the development of family and tribe; social units bound together by emotion rather than just instinct.

And as primates developed into humans we developed the cerebral cortices, overlapping the limbic system that overlapped the reptilian brain. This gave humans an increased ability to perceive themselves and to understand themselves and their emotions. This enables us to think about the past and the future, to consider options, and to have an abstract and conceptual awareness.

Our brains are so complex that they can create distance between our direct experience and what we think about. We can get so focused on what we are thinking about that we neglect basic survival instincts. Have you met people that are so mental, so identified with their brains that they neglect their physical bodies, seem awkward and oblivious to physical reality?

Much of the focus in conscious sensuality is to reconnect us with our sensations and emotions. The work literally brings us "back to our senses," so we can experience them directly. This will enable us to create new neural pathways so we can experience life more richly, entailing new choices, freedom of thought and action.

Just as reptiles and mammals can be conditioned and controlled by manipulation of instincts, people can be controlled by their emotional needs. But because we have a neocortex, we have an expanded ability to control ourselves. If we don't utilize that ability, we set ourselves up for repression and misery.

If you lock a reptile in a room without food or water, the reptile is not going to get upset, he will just be hungry and thirsty. If you lock a dog in a room without food or water he will become fearful and react to that fear with sounds and behavior designed to bring food and water, while releasing his emotion. If you lock a man in a room without food or water, he will get hungry and thirsty, then—in response to his fear of starvation—he will either get creative or, less adaptively, start to blame someone for his condition.

What is Addiction?

When our basic needs are met, we may set an intention to meet the needs of others. There is obviously more to life than having power over others. Yet so much of modern life is focused around just that. The accumulation of money enables us to get our needs met indirectly and to get people to do things for us.

What do we really want when we are in pursuit of money? What needs are we trying to meet? Why would someone become obsessed with making money to the exclusion of meeting his or her needs directly? In my mind, this obsession with money has occurred because people have become disconnected from their basic needs for connection and love, trust and respect. Money can give us the illusion of meeting these essential needs, but can never truly meet them. The pursuit of an illusion that can never truly satisfy is the root cause of addiction.

An addiction is a behavior that results from an activity that *stimulates* rather than *satisfies* a need. It is an endless behavioral loop, a hell of disconnection and isolation.

Rats in a cage do not choose to push the button to deliver more cocaine to them until they die. They are conditioned to do so. They are mere creatures of instinct.

Humans, on the other hand, do have a choice. We are autonomous beings possessing free will with the ability to choose, and thus develop personal freedom and make decisions that serve our needs and goals, rather than act on addictions.

When, as with SET, we utilize sensation and emotion to increase our consciousness, we expand our awareness in various ways. This expanded awareness, in turn, can increase both our personal happiness and our ability to support and contribute to the happiness of others.

When we escape the trap of scarcity thinking, we can look for creative ways to ensure everyone gets their needs met. Once we open our minds in this way, we can begin working together cooperatively. And that can reveal a the surprising, delightful possibility of get our basic needs met and our self actualization needs as well. This is the beauty of being human.

When we take time to directly experience our sensations we begin to rewire our brains, creating new neural pathways for joy, intimacy, and personal freedom. This is why it is so beneficial to verbalize our experience and describe our sensations without judgment or interpretation. Once we identify the sensation—verbally or inwardly, we may become aware of corresponding or connecting emotions or thoughts. Describing the sensation itself increases our chances of identifying these related thoughts and feelings and leads to better understanding of self and other. As a result we have more choice in how we respond. Said simply: the more we connect with ourselves, the more we can connect with others.

Moreover, when we experience sensation in the moment, purely, without thought of the past or the future, we can truly experience it and more easily let it go rather than distance from the sensation by thinking about it, assigning it meaning, or imagining we've experienced something other than what is actually occurring.

Pain is relatively easy to deal with if it is minor and temporary. What is more difficult is when the pain is strong and perceived as permanent. The *fear* of pain, the emotion, is often more difficult to deal with than the *experience* of pain, the sensation. If I am in pain and believe it will go away, it is not so painful. In contrast, the fear of future pain when we are not experiencing pain in the moment can be excruciating.

I used to have re-occurring boils or skin eruptions. Whenever I would get stressed out and fearful, or have too much stimulation or heat, my body would react with mini-volcanoes of red hot, swelling boils. I was living in Hawai'i at the time, just miles from the most active volcano in the world. This proximity tends to stir people up energetically; skin conditions like mine are relatively common here, unlike a cold, dry climate such as Wyoming.

But I was determined to manage this condition. I learned I could minimize these eruptions with diet, exercise, calming and cooling activities. The boils became an opportunity for increased awareness of how I am living in my body and how my thoughts and emotions affect my body.

The Difference between Feelings and Emotions

The SET process is a way to gain perspective on sensations, emotions and thoughts. So often people unconsciously describe their experiences as "feelings" when they have lumped together sensations, emotions and thoughts. The SET process is a practice whereby we pay attention to specific sensations, emotions and thoughts. We practice communicating our experiences to others, which is a practice of connecting with others in addition to connecting with ourselves.

We could just encourage people to consider their sensations, emotions and thoughts, but the act of revealing our experiences allows us to see where we are lacking in awareness and thus increase it. The act of communicating our experiences, particularly describing our sensations, is very important in distinguishing sensation from emotion. When we are adept at distinguishing sensation from emotion from thought, we are no longer held prisoner by ambiguous and amorphous "feelings."

I can get triggered when people tell me what I'm feeling. Evermore so when they attempt to convince me their projection is true. My former wife used to do this and now when it happens, I often get triggered. I am vulnerable in this situation because I default to a fear that I *do not* know what I want. On the other hand, if I am confident and connected with myself, I do not get triggered in this type of situation. Even if the other person communicates without owning their perspective, I can see that they are actually revealing something to me about themselves. From that place, I am more open and able to appreciate the gift of them sharing their perception of me.

This confidence comes from self-knowledge that one gains by doing the SET process. It is very much a personal journey. From my perspective, self-awareness is a prerequisite for healthy relationships. Those of us who crave meaningful connection with others do well to deepen our connection with ourselves. This is one of the most important distinctions in our approach to conscious sensuality: The primacy of our relationship with self.

Typically, this involves facing our demons, our doubt and self-judgment. Releasing these judgments brings out the good, the bad, and the ugly, which is why and intentional process such as Conscious Emotional Release is useful. Otherwise, when we try to connect with others, we run the risk of subconsciously trying to work through our emotions and sabotaging our effort to connect. Let me say that again: our need for emotional release is so great that we will unconsciously release emotions in ways that *inhibit* our goal of emotional connection.

When we look deeply into ourselves and speak our sensation, emotions and thoughts, we become much more aware of ourselves and this can be disturbing. We will likely judge ourselves harshly. But if we ride the tide and follow the process, we will release our judgments and relax into ourselves. This is one of the benefits of self-awareness. And because the process of release creates a positive feedback loop, we can reveal and release more, emptying ourselves of negativity and landing right where we are in the present moment.

This practice, while distinction from meditation, allows for a quiet mind were we rest in the now. In the SET process, we take the additional step of writing down or speaking our sensations, emotions, and thoughts and then letting them go. Once we are more advanced and aware we may not need to write them down or speak them aloud. But there is the danger that knowing the process intellectually will preclude the actual doing of it. This is unfortunate, because in the act of doing the work we more easily release the material than if we just think about it. By speaking or writing, we actively and energetically expel the material from within us, giving motion to the emotion. Both are physical acts – writing and speaking – and both serve to release emotions.

We often fear judgment or shame, which can prevent us from doing practices of release such as SET. We may fool ourselves into believing we do not need to actually *do* the process, and can just think about it, which may lead to more thoughts, judgments and further distance from our emotions and sensations.

When we practice speaking our truth to ourselves and to others, we gain strength and confidence. We begin to trust ourselves, trust that we know ourselves; this helps us value ourselves.

At a certain point, we need to choose whether to project an "image" to others or to reveal ourselves. In order to reveal ourselves, we must have enough self-love that we are not afraid of another's judgments. The SET process is very useful in this regard. And when we practice with others, hear them revealing themselves, connecting with their desire for truth, increasing self-love and awareness, we feel encouraged to do the same.

The Importance of Being Concise and Precise

The SET process is a practice that refines our ability to communicate. If we communicate with as few words as possible and as accurately as possible, we increase the power of our communication. It is similar to food: the name of the game in nutrition is to get as much nutrition as possible in as little food as possible. The more food we eat, the more energy we require to digest the food. So eating more nutrient-rich foods actually increases our energy and well-being. In addition, we know that eating fiber keeps our digestive system strong and clean. Metaphorically speaking, the SET process is the fiber that provides structure so that our sensations, emotions and thoughts, consciously experienced, enhance our relationships by feeding them good food.

Similar to our food choices, we do well to say more with as few words as possible. This is much more powerful because we allow space for the communication to be received. It demonstrates confidence and strength. When we speak simply and clearly, we communicate our self-knowledge to others and ourselves. A number of years ago I noticed a strange phenomena: people often say "yes" and "no" in the same sentence. Have you ever heard someone say, "Yes, no, I agree with you" or "Yes, no, I..." It sounds totally illogical, but I hear people combine yes and no quite often, sometimes throwing in a "maybe" just to confuse people even more.

I had a boss once who would combine "yes" and "no" in almost every sentence. To my way of thinking, this unconscious habit is rooted in lack of confidence, or fear about how one's words will be received. People preface statements with yes and no to say what they have to say, but not take responsibility for it.

When we actually listen to the words people say, as opposed to just unconsciously taking in what they are *trying* to communicate, our perception of them will likely change. Often people may try to slip in some judgment as a joke, or portray something very deep and serious in a light-hearted way. But pay attention to their words *and* their tone.

Importance of Tone

In our communication practices, both for connection and for release, we encourage people to speak in a neutral tone of voice. Often people mistake neutral for cold, robotic speaking, but we can talk normally as if we are not experiencing a charge. However, if you are experiencing a high level of charge, it is better to speak with a charged voice than to repress yourself. When we communicate for connection, we should not have a high level of charge. If we do, we should consider communicating for release first, then for connection.

By communicating in a neutral tone of voice, we can focus on what is being said, rather than how it is being said. This increases our conscious awareness of the material and allows us to examine what we are saying. So often, people say things and then are irritated when others do not understand them. This happens a lot with men listening to women. Women have been oppressed for so long, they are often blocked in their throats and have a hard time explicitly describing their emotions or their desires.

Women will tend to communicate more non-verbally and are frustrated when men do not pick up on non-verbal clues. While this is an over-generalization, it has been my experience that women know what emotions they are experiencing, yet have a hard time putting them into words, especially with men. On the other hand, men tend to have a harder time knowing what emotions they are experiencing but are usually more concise in their communication.

Whatever your gender, it can be a useful practice speaking with a neutral tone. When communicating for connection, speaking with a neutral tone helps the receiver/listener to more accurately take in the content of what you are saying. When communicating for release, the neutral tone encourages us to use our words to facilitate the release. And if you have a strong emotion it is more important to say it however you need to say it than force yourself to speak in a neutral tone.

Of course there are other forms of emotional release. One of my favorites is dance. Another is swimming in the ocean. Full body, creative, playful activities are very allow our bodies to unwind and move in ways that are therapeutic rather than functional. So much of our adult lives are centered around functional activities that we often lose the ability to be spontaneous and playful.

In the military, a neutral tone is referred to as "Tone 40." Tone 40 was useful to train people to convey information without an emotional charge. Say one is at war with bombs dropping everywhere. They would want to be able to convey information in a manner that would facilitate safety and cooperation. So if a missile is headed their way, rather than run around screaming, "There's a missile coming right at us! We're all going to dieeeeeee...!" they are trained to say in a neutral tone, "Sir, a missile is headed towards us."

Of course, the military is not a hotbed of emotional health. So rather than say "tone 40," I suggest a "neutral" tone of voice.

As a teenager, I worked at the Pentagon during summer and winter breaks. I got to know many military personnel and experienced first hand how emotions were discouraged. The people I met and worked with were not robotic, but there were no officially sanctioned activities that encouraged emotional release. Of course, that is also the case in most corporations, schools, and homes.

Even in the non-profit world we did no better supporting emotional health. This is partly due to the fear that expressing emotions might jeopardize one's job. But even in non-hierarchical relationships outside of work, people rarely express their emotions clearly and consciously, without a charge.

Emotions are often only expressed when the charge is so great that the pressure relief valve opens and emotions come spilling out in intense ways infused with judgments and stories. By practicing speaking our charges in a neutral way, we gain develop the ability to speak our charges in a way that others can hear them and we can hear theirs as well.

When you first start working with these practices, you may find yourself unable to speak real charges in a neutral tone of voice. That is OK; just speak your charges without repressing yourself. But I encourage you to hold an intention of speaking in a neutral tone of voice. It is not better, just more effective.

In the Conscious Sensuality communication games we play, I encourage people to be as concise and precise as possible, to delivering the information in a nutritious package, so to speak. This is the challenge and why we call it a *practice*. When we are not playing the game, our practice will serve us.

I like to reference a specific time, place and people in regard to my SET's. You can practice this by using the word sequence below:

Time/Place/Sensation/Emotion/Thought

Ideally, you will write or speak a whole SET in one sentence. Such as, "Yesterday afternoon, when you started mowing the grass, I noticed a hot, drawing sensation in my abdomen and I noticed fear when I realized I had promised you I would do it and forgot."

We will not always be aware of our sensations, emotions and thoughts in the midst of an experience. The act of speaking or writing them down may stimulate the memory of a sensation, emotion or thought that was attached to the experience but was unconscious. It will also bring sensations, emotions and thoughts to the surface of conscious awareness as an important value of the practice. By doing this we literally discover new parts of ourselves that enrich our life experience.

Here's another example of time/place/emotion, thought: "When you walk into the room, I noticed my heart beat faster and I was attracted to you." While many men cannot imagine saying this, I have found that women who are empowered and sex-positive appreciate the honesty and the fact I am sharing *my* experience, not just complimenting them, which they might perceive as a form of manipulation.

All we can truly speak of is our own experience. Even if we are convinced we are the most brilliant psychoanalyst in the world and we understand why someone is a certain way, what good does it do us, or them, to give them unsolicited opinions or advice?

Are You Communicating for Connection or Release?
The more we reveal of ourselves, the more we create space for others to discover us and build connection. It is very useful to remember what our goals are in communicating. If we are locked in a struggle where it seems more important to be right and be acknowledged as right, we are likely communicating for release and in need of empathy.

When I think back to my life with my wife and all the arguments we had, I realize I had a strong need for empathy that was not met. I believe my wife did love me. But because her own need for empathy was unmet and she was likely unaware of some of her needs, it was difficult for her to feel empathy toward me.

Of course this is *my* view of her and it is really about me, not her. The naked truth is this: I was in need of empathy and did not know how to ask for or receive it. Furthermore, and in the interest of owning my projections on her, I believe my wife didn't receive the empathy she needed from me.

I find that rather than go into a complex analysis, it is more helpful to acknowledge our truth in the present moment. When we know our truth and speak it in the present moment, we are grounding ourselves in our present experience and consciousness. No matter how we view events of the past, speaking in present time is both empowering and liberating. Often by going into a complex psychoanalysis we are distancing ourselves from present reality and building the ego by engaging in cerebral masturbation.

We are not our past experience. It formed and shaped us to be sure, but we have the freedom to choose our actions, words and beliefs in the present moment. The present is the only place where we can experience freedom; it is the most powerful place from which to operate.

And to get there we need to release the past. Many people believe, probably out of fear, that releasing the past means reliving it or wallowing in it.

In South Africa, after the fall of apartheid, Archbishop Desmond Tutu led the Truth and Reconciliation panels that heard testimony of the horrors people experienced during the past regime. This was not to justify retribution, but to *minimize the potential* of retribution and more violence. This is a large-scale example of communicating for release. After the emotions are released, after the words are spoken, there is more potential for connection.

Increase Attention Rather Than Stimulation

Increasing our attention rather than increasing stimulation, is a key goal of this approach. When we set an intention to become more aware, we increase our capacity to experience life. Just as in the food example, the more aware we are, the less it takes to satisfy us. We can be happy with simple sensations when we hone our ability to receive them.

I encourage people to utilize the the SET approach in *both* when communicating for release and communicating for connection. The distinction is our intention: are we communicating for release or connection? In both cases, the more concise and precise we can be in regard to our sensations, emotions and thoughts, the more successful we will be in achieving our goals.

When we practice the SET approach while engaged in a sexual experience, we increase our capacity for self-knowledge and communication, *outside* of sexual experiences. We are taking an evolutionary leap when we use a sexual encounter to increase awareness and connection, rather than merely for pleasure, reproduction or following a prescribed moral code.

The Bonobo chimpanzees utilize genital stimulation to release emotions and promote bonding. It is an evolutionary adaptation that fosters social cohesion and survival. We can learn much from them about using sensory enjoyment to increase our understanding of others and ourselves. The important thing is not the activity or ritual but the intention or conscious motivation that enables the activity to serve others and us.

Having a Personal SET Daily Practice

Take 10 minutes each day and write down specific experiences that happened *that* day, not in the past. Write a sentence that references specific time/place/people and the sensations, emotions and thoughts you experience. Do it line by line, sentence by sentence, and practice using as accurate and as few words as possible. When you have finished your list, read each one out loud and notice what sensations, emotions and thoughts you have as you read them and hear yourself say them.

It is important to reference only events that happened that day. If you want, when you are done, you can do a similar process for events that happened in the past. But by sticking to the immediate past, we practice staying current and not holding onto to our charges. You may find that long-standing issues or upsets may dissipate when you take time to release the current charge. In this way, we increase our ability to release our emotions and thoughts more quickly and easily.

This process serves us just as colon hydrotherapy flushes out unnecessary material from our digestive systems and allows us to take in more nutrition as it enters our bodies. Clearing out the old will allow better absorption of the new. Have you ever witnessed someone who is unappreciative of the gifts in their life, instead focusing on some past hurts? I often experienced this with my wife, who was frustrated and annoyed by my lack of gratitude. When I saw her again after 5 years of separation, she remarked how glad she was to see that I expressed more gratitude.

My work at releasing my emotions and thoughts enabled me to live more in the present moment, to enjoy life more, and to *be* more grateful. And the happier we are, the more attractive we are to others.

I am talking about revealing ourselves to ourselves, not just creating positive intentions while we are weighed down by fears, hurts and doubts. The key is to acknowledge the emotions and thoughts, release them in a conscious, efficient, graceful manner without burdening others, and then open to the mystery of what life has to offer rather than allowing our unconscious pain to drive our desires in ways that will never truly satisfy them. Otherwise, we will continue to oscillate between unconscious reaction and unconscious repression.

Moving into conscious response means we *choose* how and when to respond to our emotions. And that choice means it is not just one answer at all times that works for everyone. It is not one ideology or a rigid formula. That is why I present many different practices or exercises for you to try, without attachment to which ones you will find most useful.

Ideologism – The Unconscious Belief That Our Beliefs Will "Save" Us

There is a link between ideologies, and both self-repression and oppression of others. To initiate violence in any way—on others or ourselves—we need to have a very good reason. People in general are not comfortable with hurting themselves or others; to get people to do unnatural, harmful acts, we need to convince them there is a very good reason, usually wrapped up in morals or a "should." Without such moralistic behavior and dogma, people would not go off to war, kill strangers or harm members of their own families.

So how do we get rid of repression, oppression and violence? By cultivating our own personal power and integrity. When we cultivate our integrity we are developing our capacity to make choices for ourselves with *reference* to others. We are paying attention to people, not ideas. This enables us to perceive ourselves and make distinctions and discernments. It also builds trust, which is an antidote to fear. So empowered people of high integrity are far less likely to fall under the sway of any type of ideology.

An ideology is really a system of belief that proposes that experiences and phenomena can be reduced simplistically and that system of beliefs can be substituted for discernment and choice. Ideologies promote solutions that are *required* for a moral response. Ideologies are based on how the world *should* be, and of how we *should* act.

It does not matter where the ideologies lie on the political spectrum. Any ideology – a system of belief that substitutes ideas for individual consciousness – is a barrier to the development of an empowered, compassionate person. This is not to say there should be no rules or boundaries, but that we not lose sight of the purpose of the rules and boundaries: to serve people, the planet and other beings, rather than to maintain a rigid ideology.

Before I moved to Hawai'I there was a community on the island that took on a radically different ideology and put it into practice. They wanted to destroy the nuclear family, which they saw as the root of environmental destruction, individual oppression and repression. They lived communally, sleeping all in one room, parents, children, everyone. They adopted an ideology of polyamory, where polyamory was seen as the only moral choice: people could not stay in monogamous relationships and live in the community. They also used drugs such as marijuana and LSD very frequently in an attempt to overcome their conditioning and promote group cohesion. In many ways, they fit the mainstream media's version of a cult. They were into drugs, sex and lived communally in the jungle. They separated themselves from others who were not in the community.

I contemplated their lifestyle and belief system as I grew in consciousness and freed myself from my own oppressive value system. Their example helped me to see the danger of ideologies, even ones that may be attractive.

Ideologies are Seductive Because They Appeal to the Part of Us That *Doesn't* Want to Think

Bear in mind that I am offering up my thoughts, experiences and insight in an attempt to understand them better myself and with the intention that they be useful to you. I do not desire to create an ideology of Conscious Sensuality, nor do I want people to rigidly follow all of my suggestions. Try it out; see if it resonates with you, check out how your body, mind, and spirit responds. And notice how these suggestions affect your relationships to self and those around you.

CHAPTER 3:
The 3-Step Communication model

The work we do to develop our capacity to see and acknowledge our sensations, emotions and thoughts is key if we are to reach our communication goals. The first step is to release emotions so we can come into the present moment. The second step is to communicate our emotions and perceptions to others. Then, when we are in a place of trust and connection with others, we can make conscious decisions. This third step is where we truly empower ourselves.

Clear communication is the key to relationships. When we communicate with transparency, relationships flow easily. When we are not clear and cannot understand others, frustration, fear and distance result.

It is important to distinguish between verbal and non-verbal forms of communication. Both are important. In any significant relationship, we will communicate non-verbally at times, which helps us stay focused at the levels of sensation and emotion. A solid foundation of verbal communication is also key, allowing us to know what is going on for the other person.

We can convince ourselves that we know what another is experiencing, but without verbal communication, we have only our intuition and perception to rely on. Even the most intuitive and perceptive among us are susceptible to "mis-read" situations, to assume and project our interpretations onto others as if they were true. The solution is simple: *Ask*. It is the most effective way to connect with a partner. Ask them to describe their emotions. Ask what they are thinking and sensing. Ask them out of a curiosity to know them better and better meet their needs. People respond well when they trust that someone truly wants to see, hear and understand them.

It is crucial to distinguish between three types of communication:
   1) communicating for release/empathy,
   2) communicating for connection, and
   3) communicating for decision-making.

In my relationships and in groups of people, I have experienced how useful it is to communicate for release and empathy first. Before you can connect with someone else you must be in the present moment and this requires that you release anything that prevents you from being present. There are many ways to release and receive empathy; choose the ones that work best for you.

Once you have released your emotions and are present and clear, you are available for connection. The vast majority of people who are not having satisfying relationships are in need of emotional release and empathy. They are simply not available for connection until these needs are met.

Communicating for release is a one-way street: if you are the person releasing, you are 100% focused on your emotions. You are freed from having to give attention to your partner. You get the opportunity to dive into your feelings and experience them fully to achieve release.

If you are on the receiving end, you need to be relatively clear yourself so you can ground the charges of your partner. If you are angry with your partner or have some unacknowledged charge with them, you will not be an effective ground for their release. This is why is it so important that people in partnership relationships have other people with whom to do emotional release work.

The First Step: The Conscious Emotional Release Practice

The conscious emotional release work we practice and teach takes inspiration from several different approaches such as Re-evaluation counseling, Non-Violent Communication and the practices developed by More University.

When I take on the role of receiver in a conscious emotional release session I begin the session by saying: "We're going to do a 10 or 15- minute conscious release session. Everything you say will be confidential; I'm not going to judge you or anyone you speak about. I will allow the charges to flow through me and to the ground. Are you ready to begin?"

When the other person affirms their desire to begin, I ask, "What do you want to release to come into the present moment?" I continue to ask this question throughout the session until it is over. This enables me to drop into a meditative space where I am giving attention but not distracted by what the person has to say. I am not as likely to take on their story, agree or disagree, or give advice when I am focused on helping them release their charges.

It's important to make a verbal statement of my intention to be present and neutral during the session. It reminds me to remain in the role of witness and not participate in their stories. So often people get stuck in their past and create conflict in relationships because they hold onto their stories about other people. They become skilled at fooling themselves that the other person is to blame for their unhappiness and skilled at convincing others as well. No matter how much we may dislike something someone has done or said, it continues to hurt us when we do not release our judgment about it and the person who did it. When holding ground as a witness, we remain neutral rather than get consumed by what they should have done, why they did it, and how they should be punished.

The key question is: "Do we want to change how we relate or respond?" When we ground our charges, we take the energy of the emotion and allow it to disperse in the ground just as a house has an electrical ground. If the house is struck by lightening, the ground will take the electrical charge and safely transfer it into the Earth.

We can do a similar process with our own intense emotional charges. Setting the intention at the beginning of a session is an important step in that process. Releasing our charges and not holding them for any reason is a crucial component of this work.

We may say we want to release our charges but still blame others for our unhappiness. It is very seductive, this tendency to deny responsibility for our own happiness. In many ways, it is built into our everyday language, and thus requires intentional focus if we are to break the pattern.

It's true: people do awful things to each other. People lie, cheat, steal and sometimes rape and murder. But as long as we blame others, we give them the power to decide how we are going to respond. Blaming others is the result of an error in thinking. We think the person we blame somehow gets something over on us. When we blame others, whether for a petty infraction or something as large as mass genocide, we fail to realize that the alleged perpetrators are suffering too.

Anyone perpetrating war or violence is just as much the victim of it. No one in their right mind would create such suffering. Yes, it is awful to be a victim, but it is also awful to be the perpetrator and have to live with the knowledge of how your actions made others suffer.

It is a delusion to think that people can commit violence and crimes without impacting themselves. They may stuff it down and even claim not to be bothered by their actions, but every act devoid of integrity, love, and compassion takes its toll. Unfortunately, the mechanism of addiction often causes perpetrators to create more suffering as a way to release their repressed feelings of sadness and guilt over what they have done.

Have you ever seen a child, or an adult, get injured by some inanimate object and then watch as they release their anger on the inanimate object as if it had caused the pain? How can we transform our anger, frustration and pain so it is fully released and does not cause anyone or us pain?

To be in integrity is to be in a place of compassion and to be compassionate, we must come into integrity. This will allow us to love others and ourselves.

When we act outside of our integrity it is because of fear. We somehow convince ourselves that we need to do things to benefit ourselves at the expense of others. This perpetuates the illusion of separateness, which causes pain. And we then justify our actions with stories referencing moral justifications or ideologies.

To forgive ourselves is to acknowledge that we acted out of fear and ignorance of our underlying connection with everyone and everything. To forgive ourselves is to release blaming ourselves, which allows us to forgive others. Until we learn to forgive ourselves we cannot forgive others. This is the essence of ho'oponopono as I understand it.

Along with the verbal emotional release process described above, we use a non-verbal component. This is especially useful when the level of charge is high and the person tends to get stuck in their mind.

This exercise was developed with inspiration from Re-evaluation Counseling, Wholistic Peer Support (by Amara Wahaba Karuna), and the withhold process from the Morehouse/One Taste Community, Heart of Now/Naka Ima, the Zegg community in Germany and their Forum process, and the Human Awareness Institute, all of whom have influenced me.

The key to this exercise is its simplicity and repetition, which enables us to drop into a meditative space. This is not a process designed to help you "figure out" yourself or your issues. Our brains are good for solving math problems; not so much for figuring out emotions. It is a process to help release emotional charges and come into present time to be more in touch with our natural state of joy. Much talk therapy is useful in helping people put their lives and their issues in a context or understanding so they can gain freedom from habitual responses. But talking about our issues and difficulties often reinforces the belief that we are damaged and defined by our problems.

In this practice, we are essentially sweeping out the emotional debris we clear the decks to allow more light and air in our beings. With the support of a peer, we acknowledge emotional charges or disappointments when they come up and releasing them without judgment. By giving and receiving in this way we can see the emotional release process as "regular maintenance" that is healthy for everyone. If something needs to be processed or communicated after we achieve release, we can do so with more focus and less emotional charge.

Find a partner with whom you do *not* have a sexual relationship or emotional charges. This is important because release charges is the purpose of this exercise. Be aware of the distinction between the goal of connecting and the goal of releasing. So often people try to build connection and get emotional release at the same time, and often with a sexual partner who is confused as to how to meet their partner's needs. No wonder we have arguments!

It is best is to sit in a quiet space free from distractions and possible disruptions. You can do this over the phone, but the eye contact is useful in keeping us focused.

The Reasons for Non-Verbal Emotional Release

While the non-verbal emotional release process often employs words, the emphasis in this practice is on moving the energy out of the body. For many people they have been trained and conditioned to not physically express their emotions. Moving our bodies to consciously release our emotions is a powerful step towards reclaiming our right to have emotions and our ability to choose how to respond to our emotions.

It's important to focus on the release of emotions and keep yourself, others, and the physical environment safe from damage during your releasing. I remember during my marriage I would be so upset sometimes but unable, or unwilling, to release my emotions in a safe manner. I would do the dishes and break them as I washed. I would get triggered during a phone call and smash the phone down at the end of the call. It is embarrassing to recall these and other incidents caused by anger.

It wasn't a matter of doing a poor job of *controlling* my anger. I was simply not able to *express* my anger in a safe and effective way. Anger, I have learned, is often if not always a secondary emotion. It is a response to fear, sadness or frustration. If we can recognize, articulate and release fear, sadness and frustration, we will not be angry or at least not so angry that we do things we later regret.

Many people think that conscious non-verbal emotional release looks and feels childish. However, consider the wisdom of people around the world and how they deal with issues such as grief over losing a loved one. Traditional forms of mourning and grieving are physical and vocal expressions of loss. People wail, stomp, cry, throw their arms out, and toss their heads back to release. This is the body's wisdom.

And then compare this to a funeral in the repressed western world where people try so hard *not* to express their emotions. Which of course makes people less present and available to give each other love and support. Repression is when we use our energy to stop ourselves from feeling what we naturally feel.

My mother died in autumn. On Mother's Day the following spring, my father, sister and our families went back to our family beach home to scatter her ashes in the ocean and memorialize her life. This was the place where I saw my mother as happiest. I remember how strange it was to be back in the house, staying in the same bedroom as I did when I was young, yet this time I was married and my father was alone in the master bedroom with mom's ashes in an urn on the dresser.

At the appointed time, we all went down to the ocean to scatter the ashes. My dad carried the urn and we were in thigh deep water when my sister's husband, a lawyer like my sister and father, told my dad that scattering ashes was illegal. I think that made my dad nervous. As he poured the ashes into the surf, I began to have an intense emotional release: I became weak-kneed and staggered around wailing. I remember having the experience of ecstasy and rapture as my mother was reunited with the ocean.

My sister, very concerned, kept saying, "Are you alright, are you alright?" I was fine, and I knew it, I was just experiencing and releasing a lot of emotion. I know this helped me cope more easily with the loss of my mother.

My sister, busy with a young child and a full-time legal career, did not have as easy a time dealing with the death of our mother. She took on the role of mom in blaming and shaming and complaining about Dad. In the years following Mom's death and my dad's subsequent remarriage, my dad and sister's relationship went from good to bad to practically non-existent.

What if they had known how to express and release their emotions? The natural state of our being is love, particularly between parent and child. What disrupts this state of love is not the actions or inactions taken on either part, but the inability to release emotions associated with that person. We do not ever intend to harm or hurt anyone; behaviors are the result of unconscious and unexpressed emotions.

Non-Verbal Conscious Emotional Release Practice

You can do this exercise alone, with a partner and as part of your verbal session as well. Set the intention to release your emotions and to keep everyone and everything safe. Breathe deeply and rapidly, as this will bring emotion to the surface.

Hit pillows. This is a good way to express emotions. Hit the pillows with open palms and with your forearms in a rhythmic way. Do not try to damage the pillows, just focus on breathing, moving your body and releasing.

Wail. Expressing sadness and grief can be done by throwing your arms out to the side, tilting your head back and letting out sound.

Hand-scream. If you feel a desire to scream and do not want to upset other people, simply cup your hands over your mouth. Scream from your belly so you do not hurt your throat.

Stomp. Stomping up and down with awareness can help release and ground the emotional energy as your legs and feet contact the floor or ground.

Tantrum. Lay back and move your head and body from side to side and stomp your feet and hit your palms on the bed or the floor.

Go Fetal. When you are too depressed to do any of the above, curl up into a tight fetal ball and push all your air out. Keep the air out as long as possible and when you do breathe, open up your body completely. Do this at least 3 times. This will connect you with your body and brain's will for life and release tension and fear.

There are a number of group activities and exercises for emotional release and empathy as well. While the exercises hopefully result in more love, trust and connection in the group, what distinguishes these activities from connection exercises is that they encourage the development of our witnessing and empathy skills. Developing our ability to be fully present without having to do anything when strong emotion surfaces, is valuable personally and to a relationship or group.

The Witnessing Circle

An effective ritual to dissolve fear, shame and guilt is the "Witnessing Circle." This is an opportunity to reveal oneself to oneself in the presence of others. The way it works is the group will gather in a circle and one by one, people will step into the circle to share some truths present for them in that moment.

After someone steps into the circle and speaks their truth, those who resonate or relate with what was shared join the speaker in the center of the circle. Everyone has a chance to witness who is there, then everyone rejoins the circle. One after the other, people go into the center and reveal something. Witnessing people silently release in this way helps to ground the energy.

It is important to use the practice as an opportunity to see ourselves in the context of others. Sometimes people will experience a desire to step into the center to comfort someone even though they did not experience or could not relate to what was shared. Beware of doing this because people often do this as a way of unconsciously releasing something that was stirred up in them but *not* acknowledged.

This is another important way to practice seeing everyone as strong and capable. When we are uncomfortable and try to give comfort to someone who is not requesting it, we diminish them in our eyes and ignore our own needs. When we notice a desire to comfort someone it is important to ask them, "What can I do for you?" or "How can I support you?" This lets them know we are available, we care, *and* that we see them as capable of asking for what they need. This simple act of seeing another as capable and strong can help that person tremendously, by encouraging them to see *themselves* as strong enough to ask for what they want.

The focus in the Witnessing Circle is to be as concise and precise as possible. It is important to speak in complete sentences, with reference to oneself, a specific time/place, what occurred, and the emotions experienced.

It becomes a beautiful dance of flowing and ebbing, into the center and out of the center, with a different group each time resonating with each experience.

Sometimes an individual wants to say something light and humorous, or make a statement everyone can relate to when they step into the center. This can be effective at helping people open up, but it can inhibit deeper shares as well. By cultivating our ability to witness without judging, we increase our ability to empathize and our ability to release consciously.

ZEGG Forum

The ZEGG community in Germany practices a similar type of group process. ZEGG, a German acronym for Center for Experimental Culture, was created in the 1970's when a group of young people, inspired by professor and author Dieter Duhm, sought to put into practice the values of pacifism, ecology and social and economic justice. They realized at some point fairly soon, that they could not reach their goals and resolve their issue without addressing issues of the heart.

They called the process they developed the forum. They held the forum almost every day and it became a focal point of the community. This forum was a place to see and be seen, and to release emotions present in people. It became significant glue that held the community together. Certain community members became exceptionally skilled at facilitating the process. Today, two of them, Ina and Achim, travel the world teaching and facilitating the process.

Not surprisingly, much of the material that comes up during the forum has to do with love, relationships, and sexuality. In fact, ZEGG, and their sister community Tamera in Portugal, have been leaders in the realm of conscious relationships and open sexuality. They realized that as long as significant blocks existed in people's hearts and sexuality, it would not be possible to create a more cooperative culture and reach their goals of ecology, peace, and justice.

In the ZEGG forum, someone who is moved to present some material about him- or herself will stand up and enter the center of the circle. They will describe, in their own words and style, what is up for them. Often little needs to be said and they are complete. Other times, there is a lot that needs to be released and it may even involve another member standing up and joining the speaker in the center to help guide and facilitate them.

One of the practices of ZEGG forum is to keep moving. The ZEGG people noticed that moving the body is one of the best ways to keep the emotions flowing toward release and resolution. Facilitators will take participants by the hand, encourage them to keep walking, running, dancing or in some way move their body to release emotion. They may even suggest an action to dramatize the emotion rather than just stand there and using words.

One of the aspects of ZEGG forum is the opportunity to give the speaker a "reflection" or a "mirror" when they are done presenting. This is a chance for one of the witnessing community members to get up and share what they saw. The idea is to give a reflection that is useful to the person who presented, not a chance to release his or her own material that may have been stimulated. Reflections are designed to keep attention on the person who just finished, and give them insight or another perspective on their material.

The Second Step: Communicating for Connection

Once we release our emotions and connect to ourselves we are available to connect with others. In this state we are naturally curious about others and desire closeness and understanding. Communicating for connection is a two-way street, unlike the one-way street of release. When communicating for connection we give and receive, listen and talk, build intimacy, trust, understanding and love.

Ideally, most of the time we communicate with our lovers we communicate for connection. This is what feeds us. If we notice that we are not connecting easily, it could be that we need to communicate for release and empathy first. Be aware that communicating for release and empathy with a lover or partner may be difficult or may dull the love and passion.

This is not to say that one should hide their need for release from their lover but that it is more effective in building love, trust and connection to release the charge to someone other than our lover in most cases. Once the intensity of the charge has been released, the information can be conveyed to our lover. This does not decrease intimacy or honesty; it is simply a more effective manner to release the charges and a better way of supporting the intimacy and sexual charge with a lover.

Once we start complaining regularly to a lover, we will notice a marked drop-off in sexual attraction and energy. Another good reason not to do emotional release work with a lover is that we may have significant charges with him or her that could more easily be released when an objective person hears those charges.

It is good to choose someone who cares about us and supports our relationship. Too often people pick someone they feel a sexual attraction to and use the release process to build intimacy with this person. Obviously, this may end up compromising intimacy with our lover and both sacrifice that relationship and sabotage the possibility of a new relationship.

There will be times when our need for release is so great, the only person to work with is our lover or a desired lover. In this case, it is important to be aware of how we may be hiding our truth, or trying to manipulate or impress the listener.

There are many ways we can build trust, love and intimacy with someone. Sharing about ourselves and asking questions about the other are ways we get to know someone and deepen our connection.

Entering The Spotlight

In some ways ZEGG forum is similar to a practice we call "Spotlight" in Conscious Sensuality workshops. "Spotlight" is similar to the game many people know as "Hot Seat" or, alternatively, "Love Seat." In Spotlight, the name of the game is to have one person take the spotlight and reveal themselves in detail to the group. Usually we encourage each person to give a little monologue, perhaps just for one minute at the beginning of their spotlight. This gives them a chance to get comfortable, articulate what they feel at the present moment and describe some personal issue that is in their consciousness.

After they introduce themselves and their issue or issues, members of the circle ask questions. We encourage everyone to keep attention on the person in the spotlight at all times. We encourage them to ask questions that are about the person in the spotlight and not to redirect the attention of the group to themselves. We encourage people to be mindful of their reasons or motivation for asking questions. Generally it is not helpful to make statements that are really judgments or advice cloaked in question form, but rather to ask questions from a place of compassionate curiosity. It is by staying focused on the other person that builds understanding and connection.

My understanding of compassion includes challenging the person in the spotlight, encouraging them to get to a deeper level of understanding and self-knowledge. Challenges are most effective when they come from the desire to assist the person, not from a place of strong emotion for the questioner, and not as a strategy or a manipulation to get the person in the spotlight to have a release. Some groups use processes where strong challenges are seen as valuable in a way to "break down" the other person so they can see their issues and become more honest. As in other practices, in the Spotlight exercise, we encourage people to speak as concisely and precisely as possible. Long, complicated questions are usually not questions; they are judgments, advice or self-reflections cloaked as questions.

It is more valuable to witness an individual honestly share what they see rather than manipulate them into having an emotional release. While they may have a release, if their unique process is not held with respect, the individual is less likely to trust the process and the people offering reflection. Without that trust, the release may be, in part, related to the fear that arises when we feel manipulated or sense—perhaps vaguely or subliminally—someone's manipulative energy.

If I am triggered by something someone says in Spotlight, I have an opportunity to speak it during the Revelations process, which may follow the Spotlight ritual. In Revelations, everyone takes a turn at speaking and revealing something about themselves. By sharing our hearts directly with someone, we practice building trust and intimacy. And we set an intention to suspend our desire to categorize the revelations as "positive" or "negative."

The Practice of Revelations

In Revelations, we simply share, with reference to our emotions and ourselves, what emotions are stimulated by another person.

The language for the process goes like this:
Giver: "Person A (receiver), May I reveal myself to you?"
Receiver: "Yes" or "No"
If yes, the Giver gives their revelation, referencing a specific moment/time/place and the emotions they experienced. When the Giver has finished the receiver acknowledges the revelation and says "Thank you."

It's crucial that permission be asked so that the communication can build connection, trust, and understanding.

While many people have a hard time initially with the language and the structure, it helps to create a ritual space to share things that are often difficult to share in less formal ways. It also helps to keep a structure so that people can more easily see that revelations are *about* the person speaking, not the person being spoken to. By slowing down the exchange with the set language and format, we get a chance to tune into what is actually being said and revealed.

The revelation process is a process of communication for connection, not one of emotional release. While strong emotions may be present, I encourage people to speak from a desire for connection, rather than use the opportunity to release their own emotions. If one is unable to feel their desire to be more connected and is only aware of anger or frustration, it is better to release their charge first within the container of an emotional release session. This is not to repress those with strong emotions but to practice speaking in ways that actually build trust and connection.

If I feel angry or frustrated with someone I might share it in this way: "When you did such and such, I was angry and frustrated because I couldn't understand why you did it. I want to understand you and experience trust and connection with you."

In this way, I speak my truth, revealing it to the person in question, and I reference myself in a way that enables this person to hear my desire and my emotions rather than feeling blamed for how I feel. If the perception of blame is stirred in the receiver it is likely rooted in self-judgment.

It is crucial to note that a very important aspect of a revelation is that it references the emotion of the speaker. By acknowledging our emotion we "reveal" ourselves and build more trust and understanding from the listener. If we don't include or acknowledge our emotions, it is more likely to be heard as a judgment, which can be be more difficult for the listener to hear and integrate.

The Practice of Feedback

Another communication for connection ritual is the practice of feedback. In this ritual we notice we have a perception of another person and we offer to give it to them as a gift. The ritual is very similar to the revelations ritual in that we first ask permission to give the feedback. This is crucial because it gives the receiver a chance to pause and check in if they are available and present, able to hear and integrate another's perception of them at this moment and from this person. If they cannot trust that the feedback is coming from a true desire to be helpful, they won't be able to integrate it, so there is no point in giving it. If we perceive someone has a strong emotion attached to giving their feedback, it is best to do the emotional release work first and then give the information as a revelation. What distinguishes feedback from a revelation is that there is little or no emotion attached to it.

The ritual may sound like this:

"May I give you my perception of you?"
"OK"
"I have a sense that you are afraid of intimacy and commitment in your relationship with Ilena."
"Thank you."

Or it could be statements such as:

"I see a workaholic pattern in you."
"You seem sad to me right now."
"I have a sense that you have some emotional material with your father that is impacting your relationship."

Feedback can often stir emotions just as revelations can. It's best to pause, breathe and give some space and time to integrate them as well.

One of the paradoxes is that we often see quite deeply into our sexual partners and yet, due to the emotions present, find it difficult to give or receive feedback without an emotional filter. This is why it is so beneficial to expand our circle of intimacy beyond our sexual relationships and do the emotional clearing work so we can give our lovers our feedback in a way that builds love, trust and understanding.

Judging and Being Vulnerable

We are most sensitive to perceptions of judgment from others when we are unconsciously judging ourselves. If we receive a direct judgment that is not in line with our self-judgments, we may be saddened or confused, but unlikely to respond with anger. Of course, when we do judge other people or ourselves, we are often ashamed to admit we have judgments.

I have a very clear memory of an incident that occurred when I was living at a particular community that demonstrates how difficult it can be to see and admit that we are, at times, judgmental. I had had a difficult relationship with one of the community members, an older woman I had relative fondness for, but little emotional connection with. In some ways, both physically and energetically, she reminded me of my mother. Like most of us, my relationship with my mother was complex, a mixture of enjoyable and challenging emotions, like most parent-child relationships.

At that point in my personal growth, self-empowerment, and healing, I took it as an article of faith that I should share my truth with everyone. Further, I took on the belief that revealing my true emotions and judgments would help me and build intimacy and trust within the community. I discussed this with a community member, noting the fact that just sharing my truth did not necessarily result in greater trust and intimacy in my relationship with this particular woman.

I shared that I had judgments about her physical appearance and health. These judgments stemmed from her similarities with my mother, a 2 pack a day smoker who was overweight, ate mostly processed foods and drank alcohol on a daily basis. Add to this her depressed state and her difficulty expressing emotions, and it is no wonder she died at a relatively young age from cancer. This was painful for many reasons: Losing a parent is hard enough, but I saw that, in many ways, my mother's death was hastened by the fact that she had little emotional intelligence, which contributed to her to the behaviors that destroyed her health. Try as I might to encourage my mother to adopt healthier lifestyle, she remained steadfast on her chosen course.

I loved my mother and saw the many great qualities she embodied. She was very loving and supportive of me. Even though I see how her fears drove her actions and thoughts and how she attempted to manipulate me when I was younger, I never questioned her love for me and her desire for me to be happy. Her death was a wake up call that compelled me to look at myself, my patterns, and the habits that were not serving me.

I find it funny that I was always somewhat conscious, probably more conscious than most, about my health. While I did my share of drinking alcohol and smoking pot in my days at the University of Virginia, I was never a habitual drinker and generally have had what I consider good health habits. I became a vegetarian after college when I moved into a shared house in Berkeley, California. I was an avid bicyclist and runner for years. Still and yet my mother was very concerned about me smoking marijuana when I was a senior in high school.

At the time I had not ever smoked pot, but I had a wild girlfriend with purple hair and self-destructive patterns who liked to drink and get high. I did not take on her habits, rather I took on the role of her healer. My mother though was very opposed to marijuana smoking, probably because it was completely illegal at the time.

Unbeknownst to me, I had dragged my feelings about my mother into my relationship with the woman in my community. All the feelings of disappointment, abandonment, all of my judgments about her choice to dig herself an early grave, had spilled over into my relationship with her.

When I revealed this to her, I did so from a desire to increase the trust and intimacy between us. I thought I was doing a "good thing" by supporting our relationship and community. Showing a part of myself I did not necessarily like but was willing to share made me feel vulnerable. Exposing my judgmental side to her and another community member was, in my mind, a vulnerable act. I did not try to convince anyone to adapt my judgments, I merely acknowledged them. I viewed this kind of vulnerability as a strategy to build connection, intimacy, and trust in our newly formed community. But it backfired. Just because I took it as an article of faith that I "should" be vulnerable and share my judgments of myself and others didn't mean they subscribed to that belief. And I had a big judgment about that. When I shared that in the community—revealed that I judged them as less likely to be vulnerable in this way, I become something of an emotional scapegoat for the community. At least that was my experience.

In retrospect, I believe this dynamic was a re-enactment of the dynamic between my parents . I grew up watching my mother habitually blame my father, who would simply take it without defending himself. This planted a seed in me and I developed a tendency to blame myself when difficulties arise in relationships. I believe this tendency sets up a pattern that encourages others to blame me when they are unwilling or unable to take responsibility themselves.

Embracing the Shadow

I could not understand this issue of vulnerability. I saw how I shared my "shadow" side, my vulnerability, and yet it *did not* bring me closer to others in the community. It did bring me closer to myself though and this is the key reason to be honest with others.

Growth is not as much about your relationship with others as the primacy of the relationship with yourself. By sharing my shadow or vulnerabilities with my community I was going into a deeper, more intimate relationship with myself. Ultimately this led me to a place where I now have much more intimate, trusting relationships with others, but first I needed to be honest with myself and make my honesty a priority *above* my relationships with others.

People do not often like to see our shadow side. That is why we are taught at an early age to hide it. And there may be good reasons *not* to share our shadow with others at all times. When people are in a place of emotional distress or fear, they have less capacity to allow others to show their shadow or vulnerabilities. It is similar to an empathy deficit: When someone is fearful they are less able to hold space for another's process and are more likely to react to such sharing with their own judgments.

Could people not see that I was opening myself up to criticism as a means to create more trust and harmony? Why did everyone gravitate towards the opinions and align with the other male of the group who I judged unwilling to reveal himself? The other man of our small community had lived in community for much of his adult life and had spent many years with the aforementioned community that espoused polyamory, total income sharing, and frequent use of marijuana and LSD.

I felt frustrated that he would never share his judgments as "judgments." He would not acknowledge his shadow side or be "vulnerable" as I understood the term. When I considered my actions and his, and the results, I stopped using the term "vulnerable" because in my mind, it became synonymous with inviting attack. Now, rather than be vulnerable, I set my intention on being transparent, honest and open.

Now, rather than be vulnerable and hope to build trust and be appreciated for my honesty, I make discernments about who I can be transparent, honest and open with at what times and in what settings. I am not in less integrity, but I am more aware that there are better times, places, methods, and people with whom to share deeply.

Discerning with Whom to Develop Intimacy

I believe some people have more ability to be present and understand the motivation behind my sharing. And I am less likely to go to a place of deep honesty and intimacy with someone I perceive as less able to hold a neutral space, a space without judgment. I am more likely to share deeply with those who are conscious of their own judgments and has set an intention to be aware of them.

I now have a much more finely tuned sense of the difference between communicating for release versus for connection. Of course, there is often a mix of the two in practice. When we are communicating deeply we feel a lot of trust and connection, we are more likely to experience release and healing. But this is more possible when we strengthen our practices of conscious emotional release.

When I shared the truth of my judgments with the community member that reminded me of my mother, I was very disappointed when she went into emotional reaction and further distanced herself from me. I imagine she did not feel safe in opening herself to me, and could not get past her hurt. I do not think she could see that I shared out of a desire for connection. Rather, she took that sharing as me telling her what was wrong with her.

When we are conditioned to receive that type of judgment it can be difficult to hear it as anything more than just judgment. When we judge ourselves we are more likely to be sensitive to being judged by others. When the judgment we fear is openly acknowledged it can undermine rather than build trust by reinforcing our fear-based stories. We end up closing the door on someone who cares enough to be honest.

We all have judgments, and I have learned to be more much trusting of those who openly acknowledge their judgments. I am wary around those who are ignorant of their judgments, evermore so around those who believe they are above judgments.

This brings up the difference between judgment and discernment. Judgment is when we have an opinion that references or is justified by our personal morality. Discernment is when we consciously acknowledge our perceptions and make choices with reference to ourselves rather than an external framework of morality.

The Third Step: Communicating for Decision-Making

Once you are connected with yourself in the present moment, having released your emotions, and you are in a state of connection with others you are ready to make decisions. Life is full of decisions, some big, some small and some life-changing. We make decisions all day long: what to do, when to do it, how to do it, and with whom. When we are in a state of connection to our purpose and ourselves and are connected to others, we make decisions easily. This is not just the self-focused executive who only cares for himself but also the executive who prioritizes what he wants in light of the needs of others. Why? Because when we are in a natural, connected state, we want other's needs to be met. That helps to meet our desire for contributing to the well-being of the community around us.

The first step in decision-making is acknowledgment of desire. What do you want to do? Decisions are made for more easily when we have expressed and released our emotions and are in a state of connection with ourselves. At those times, decisions flow naturally as there is no resistance or fear that impedes the process. When we are harboring unexpressed emotions, our decisions are likely to be subconsciously driven in an attempt to address these emotional needs. And since this is a subconscious process, the decisions are likely to be poor ones just as a child who is upset is less rational and makes poor decisions.

One of the things that most often gets in the way of making good decisions is difficulty in acknowledgment of desire. We are often so conditioned and repressed that desire is bad, that we try to justify our decisions in ways that minimize or don't recognize our desire. We often seek to subconsciously manipulate others by convincing them our decisions are altruistic. As much as we may try to convince others our decisions are made this way, we end of fooling and confusing ourselves and creating more separation from those we love.

There is nothing wrong with saying, "This is what I want" and "This is my desire." These are powerful statements and we are much more likely to get what we want when we clearly state it. And if there is some incongruity or lack of integrity it will come to light. What is more important than our individual preferences is our commitment to revealing the truth of our desires. By doing this, we free ourselves from the trap of unexpressed, unacknowledged desires which will be acted out subconsciously in other ways.

A crucial aspect of this is to note that it is not the mind in isolation from the body and the emotions that makes the decisions. If one makes decisions without reference to their physical body or emotional body it is from a state of disconnection and may be superficially rational but is not effective in meeting the needs of the whole person.

Wisdom in decision-making flows from a state where the mind is in deep communion with the body—a place where information is considered by the brain and felt in the body. If there are unreleased emotions, the body can't feel the information but can only make decisions with the brain, not the mind. Remember that the brain is connected to all parts of the body through the nerves that innervate every cell in our body. The brain is the decision-maker but without sensory input being processed by the brain consciously, we are making decision on the basis of our beliefs, habits and fears, not on what is actually happening in real time in our bodies.

Once you have learned how to make decisions for yourself you can move on to make decisions with other people. If you don't know how to make decisions for yourself it is impossible to make decisions with others. If you are in a place of emotional awareness and connection with yourself and have ease in making your own decisions, then you are available to make decisions with others.

The best way to make decisions with others is to simply state what we want and to ask if anyone objects. This is a powerful method that respects others by acknowledging our desire and asking explicitly for their feedback. Unfortunately, when less-empowered people hear this they can sometimes be triggered precisely because they do not have the confidence to explicitly express their desires.

When two or more people are in a decision-making mode it is crucial that everyone involved is in the present moment, without any unreleased or unacknowledged emotions and that a state of love, trust and understanding exists among the parties involved. When this is not the case, we do well to spend our time on emotional release processes and then communicating for connection using the rituals of revelations and feedback. While this may seem counter-productive or agonizingly time-inefficient, it actually saves time in the long run because later decisions will be made more quickly and those decisions will be more effective. It is also much more likely that everyone will not only agree but actively agree and support the decisions without reservations that undermine the decisions and the trust between those involved.

If someone expresses a desire or asks for support for a decision, we can do several things: agree, disagree with a different proposal, agree with a refinement, or pause. It is crucial that we do not simply disagree but express our own desire. If we do not know what we desire we should ask for a pause to go inside ourselves, meditate, release anything that is keeping us from the present moment. This pause may be 2 minutes or 2 days or 2 months.

If we suggest a different alternative or add a refinement to someone's desire or proposal we should tune in to what would meet everyone's desire. If we are in the present moment and in a state of love, trust and understanding with everyone then we naturally want to meet everyone's desires. Of course, if one is carrying hurts from the past this is very difficult to do.

Similar to revelations, it is best to express our emotions, our thoughts and own our desires rather than trying to convince or manipulate others into accepting our desires. This will build trust, even if our desires are different, and then the decision-making will flow more smoothly. It is crucial to always focus on the goals, seeing beyond personal attachment to specific strategies to meet these goals, which are often the same as everyone has the same basic needs in life.

Plausible Deniability

Often people seek to avoid responsibility for our decisions. We pretend other people make the decisions or that we were somehow ignorant of what was occurring. Plausible deniability is a legal term that means it is reasonable to believe that someone didn't know or wasn't responsible. Often in our lives, and particularly our sexual relationships, we operate from a place of plausible denial. We don't have the conversations we need to because we don't want conflict and we don't want responsibility.

If we seek to make decisions from a place of respect and without manipulation, we must acknowledge what we want and speak it.

Why We Say "Yes" When We Mean "No"

Why do we say yes when we mean no? I had a good experience of this one day. I was gardening and the phone rang. Often I just let the phone ring and check the messages later. It is important for me to choose when I answer the phone. I was gardening with a friend and enjoying it. But I had placed a call and left a message to be called back. So when the phone range I went to look to see who was calling and it was my friend who I left the message for a little while before.

I answered it and my friend proceeded to ask me to do a favor. I told her I was in the middle of gardening and I would do it later. She persisted and asked me again. I felt frustrated and annoyed and I said, "Ok, I'll go and do it now." My truth was that I did not want to do it, but I decided to do it rather than continue to have the conversation. I am sure she could sense my irritation and the call ended with both of us annoyed even though I had done the favor explicitly to try to make things better between us.

I realized that I could have said no and just dealt with the emotions she would have to my "no." Instead, I got off the track of following my desire, which resulted in my irritation and put me off-balance. And then when she was upset I was out of balance and not as available for her emotionally. I needed empathy and could not give it to her. For quite a long period in my life, I would unconsciously say yes to whatever was asked of me. I would say yes but mean no, and I would be resentful. And angry. And frustrated. With others, and myself.

Yet I would say yes, hoping I would be rewarded for my yes. When I was not living my truth, I gained little or nothing from saying yes. It took me a long time to recognize that when I thought I was being a nice guy, I was not being nice. I was being weak. By not expressing my truth I was trying to manipulate others into liking me.

That is at the core of it: when we do not say or live our truth, we participate in a dishonest attempt at manipulation of ourselves or others. And that is why it does not feel good or benefit us. When we say Yes but mean NO, it is not because we are nice, it is be cause we are afraid of what the other person will do to us or what we will experience if we say no.

CHAPTER 4:
The Role of Touch

In our workshops and trainings, people have an opportunity to bring more awareness to the art of giving and receiving touch. So often touch becomes an unconscious reflex. In sexuality, touch is often used as a strategy to build excitement but often is not experienced as a means to increase consciousness and connection.

We teach that touch has three main aspects: Location, Speed, and Pressure. By referring to touch in this way, we build a language that allows the giver and receiver to communicate more accurately and thus create more pleasure.

It is important to note that these three aspects can be used to describe touching or massaging any part of the body, from the palm of your hand to your G-spot and anywhere in between.

By using this precise language, we empower ourselves to ask for exactly what we want. And by being clear we help the giver to relax into their sensations and emotions, confident that they are giving touch that is enjoyable.

It is a simple way to practice touch rather than lots of massage theory and needing to remember anatomical names and massage strokes. Many people who have never had a massage class have an intuitive sense of what touch feels good. In contrast, many massage therapists are caught in their minds and give touch that is technically correct but insensitive and not enjoyable.

I took a few basic massage classes and then practiced a lot before I got my license. Practicing helped me focus on developing my sense of touch and learn basic body mechanics and strokes. Then after I was grounded in my ability to give touch and sensitive to what others wants, needs and experiences, I went to massage school and learned more theory and anatomy. But there is no substitute for developing the intuitive, tactile aspect of massage.

The Elbow to Fingertip Practice

This is a practice we often do in our workshops that helps in practicing the 3 aspects of touch while creating a boundary of location that begins at the fingertips of one hand and ends at the elbow. This boundary is key, for by drawing a clear boundary, both the giver and receiver relax and play within the constructed boundary. The boundary is clear that there is to be no genital touch, no breast touch and no touch on any area of the body outside of the fingertip to elbow range.

This range allows and encourages more exploration and more sensual touch than one may allow oneself without a boundary. One of my teaching partners likens it to a playground where kids will range all over the area as long as the perimeter has a fence or some boundary. When the perimeter has no fence or is unclear, kids tend to congregate in the center and do not explore as much or range as far.

So in this practice, play with the three aspects of touch and see what brings you the most pleasure as giver and receiver. Taking turns being the receiver and giver allows one to fully drop in to the experience rather than being distracted by mutual simultaneous touch.

When I give, I like to hold the receiver's elbow in the palm of my hand, laying their forearm on top of mine. Then I can use my other hand to touch and massage them while they completely relax. By holding the elbow I also reinforce the boundary for them and for me.

Expanding the Range of Sensation

It is fun to see how close you can come without making actual skin-to-skin contact and developing our perceptions of awareness in this way. To increase the levels of sensation try closing your eyes if you are the receiver.

It is important to alter each of the aspects while maintaining consistency with the other two elements. You can then focus on the most creating the most pleasure in the range with that particular aspect. For example, you might want to explore varying the speed of your touch. Keep the location and pressure the same. Just vary the speed from no speed to very fast and every speed in between. You can do the same with pressure: go from the lightest pressure possible to the point where the receiver asks for less pressure. This exercise builds trust and connection; when a receiver says the pressure is too deep or painful, I can trust that they like the amount of pressure I'm using the rest of the time.

Of course there are other things to consider when giving touch such as your intention and what part of your body you are touching them with. You can give amazing touch with more than just your hands. In Lomilomi massage we use our forearms, which are good for giving medium to deep pressure over a larger area at one time. Forearm strokes are easy on the giver as well and prevent you from overusing and straining your fingers and thumbs. Consider using the heel of your palm, your elbows and knees, your feet and even the top of your head.

Using other parts of your body such as your hair, your lips and mouth, breasts and even the genitals can create more erotic energy. Just remember if these parts of your body are too erotic you can use other parts of your body such as your hands and fingers in ways that are pleasurable and allow the receiver to relax.

Whether the touch is a BDSM-style flogging or very slow tantric lovemaking, or any other type of sensual or sexual interaction, it is all consensual and all has the potential to provide pleasure and awareness for the giver and receiver.

Levels of Intimacy and Finding your Edge

One of the key concepts in conscious sensuality is awareness of the appropriate level of intimacy. So often in life and relationships we may be unconscious of the level of intimacy and this can result in emotional upsets of fear, anger and sadness. As human beings we all want touch and pleasure. We also want safety, autonomy and respect. The key is to understanding levels of intimacy, be attuned in each moment to the truth of our being and each other and the ability to communicate with each other.

So often, instead of tuning in to ourselves and each other, we make assumptions, go unconscious, and try to meet other needs such as emotional release through our touch and physical intimacy. It's worth remembering that intimacy, sensuality and sexuality are distinct but related. We can have emotional intimacy that does not involve any touch. Many people seek to meet their needs for emotional release through touch and sexuality. Using sex for emotional release is ineffective because without conscious awareness of the process of release, the release is usually temporary. It does not address the patterns that caused the emotional disturbance. Sex for emotional release may be cathartic and powerful but it may not result in bonding, trust, and more subtle levels of pleasure that stimulate the whole being.

An easy way to understand levels of physical intimacy is to have two people face each other and have one person remain standing while the other person walks toward them. If you are sensitive, you can perceive shifts energetically as the person gets closer to you and passes each level of intimacy. The distances vary from person to person and in each situation. The key is to recognize when a level has been reached and to pause and feel the difference. Otherwise, one may be in a much deeper level of physical intimacy than is desired or an experience that cannot be integrated. When this happens, you may dissociate and start to lose connection with yourself, your body, your emotions, your mind. You may daydream or feel fuzzy or hazy.

By pausing at each point or deeper level of physical intimacy, we have an opportunity to deepen our connection with ourselves, our bodies, and our emotions. And by communicating what's happening and asking for exactly what we want, we increase our empowerment and our ability to connect on a deeper level. When this is experienced and understood, the goal is not deeper physical intimacy but deeper connection and ease in our bodies.

The Power Spot Ritual

One of the most powerful exercises we do in conscious sensuality courses is the power spot ritual. Power spots are the places on the body that hold emotional charges, memories, and are useful in helping people to release their charges and come into the present moment.

These are places that hold and store memories of unexpressed emotions such as sadness, anger, fear and others. By making contact with these areas we activate the energy or memories stored in them. This contact can be done in several ways: 1) with intention or the power of mind with no use of the hands or other body parts, 2) with the hands floating above the power spot and not making physical contact, 3) with the hands resting directly over the power spot either with clothing between the hands and the body or without.

These three ways follow the concept of levels of intimacy and the goal is to find a level that allows the receiver to feel safe and comfortable with so they can experience increased awareness and energy. Each of these forms of contact have value; one is not necessarily better than another. At different times and with different people, we choose the type of contact that seems most appropriate. If a receiver is nervous or has trust issues, it is important to communicate very clearly before there is any touch whatsoever.

When doing the power spot ritual, start by coming into a meditative position without any physical contact. Both the giver and receiver should close their eyes and drop into meditation. While breathing deeply and slowly, notice if anything is coming up in your field of awareness. Sensations, emotions, memories, thoughts, whatever is present and should be acknowledged. Stay in meditation to allow your consciousness to settle and become grounded. When you feel grounded and present, open your eyes and face your partner.

Silently gaze in each other's eyes for a few minutes. Notice any thoughts, emotions or sensations that arise. When you are ready, communicate about the session you are doing.

I suggest the giver ask questions such as:
Do you have any boundaries for the session or areas of your body that are sensitive I shouldn't touch?
Do you have an intention for the session?
Will you tell me if you want a pause or a stop to the session?
Is there anything you need to say to feel more trust and connection with me?

Take the time to thoroughly discuss whatever needs to be discussed before going into physical contact. While it may take time, it enables the receiver to drop into a much deeper place and receive much more fully. You should allow for at least 30 minutes, ideally 60 minutes for this ritual.

The power spots are: the feet, the genitals, the belly, the middle of the chest, the third-eye point a little bit above the point between the eyebrows, the top of the head, the occipital ridge at the base of the skull and top of the neck, the sacrum. All these places have the potential to bring up strong emotions and memories. It is useful to remember and remind the receiver that the point of this exercise to access these strong emotions and memories.

So often, we block ourselves from experiencing emotions and memories without even realizing it. By going slowly, paying attention and encouraging activation of the emotional body, we provide an opportunity to access and release whatever is keeping us from being in the present moment and being in our natural state of joy.

I usually start and end with the feet as it is a less intimate part of the body and it is useful to ground the receiver by focusing their attention on their feet. Before I hold their feet I close my eyes, check in with myself making sure I am present and set an intention to be helpful to the receiver. When my hands approach their feet I pause several inches away so that I can become sensitized to their energy body. This is also known as the pranic body. For some people this can be highly activating as it can create a magnetic resonance between the two bodies. I will stay in this position of floating above the physical body until my intuition tells me it is time to make physical contact.

When I make physical contact with the feet I let my hands settle onto the feet in a firm but relaxed manner. Once my hands are in this position I don't move them again until I lift off and disengage from this power spot. This is not a massage so there is no movement, no change in pressure, just solid, consistent touch that brings energy and awareness to this part of the body. I follow my intuition and may have my hands on their feet for 5 minutes or 50 minutes. If they are having an emotional release or I sense a lot of energy is moving through them, I stay present and connected to their feet until the experience subsides and is integrated.

I suggest you start with the feet because it is a great place to begin this practice, which is one of being in deep meditation with yourself while simultaneously being in physical connection with, and sensitive to, another person. This practice can have profound results in terms of creating more trust and ease between two people. It is also an opportunity to practice pausing while in a session, lovemaking, or any type of interaction.

Of course, unless you are practicing with a person you feel very comfortable with, you may not want them to touch you on some of the power spots. This is why the levels of physical intimacy are so important. You can access and focus on each of the power spots either through direct physical contact, energetic connection with the hands very close to but not touching, or simply with the mind and power of intention and visualization.

In fact, some people may have stronger responses and results with less physical contact. This is why pausing is so important. This practice is designed to create awareness and ease at each level of physical intimacy.

It is important when you break physical contact to make a clean disengagement. So often when people touch there is a sense of clinging or remaining energetically connected. So when your hands are lifting off them for the last time in the session make sure it is with the intention of clean disengagement. Do not touch them again until the session is over and they have explicitly asked for a hug or some other contact.

Expanding the Range of Sensation and Emotion: The Airbrushing Ritual

Once you have practiced the power spot exercise and intuitively and somatically understand the concept of grounding and integration, then you can move on to exercises that stimulate, activate and expand. This is a key point, for many people are in a hurry to stimulate as quickly as possible. Unless one has deeply relaxed and is in a state of trust and connection with their partner, there is a narrow range of how much one can expand energetically, sensually and sexually.

The airbrushing ritual is focused on using extremely light or non-physical touch to sensitize the body and to access the emotional body and whatever blocks may exist. This exercise is best done without clothing. As in the other touch exercises, it is important to communicate verbally and explicitly about boundaries and areas of the body you do not wish to be touched.

Just lying down naked to receive touch from another person may be beyond the level of physical intimacy one can expand into and integrate. If this is the case, you can wear clothing. A more powerful choice could be to take all your clothing off but remain covered by a sheet or sarong without receiving any physical touch.

The point is not to cause distress but to find where the blocks are and have an opportunity to bring to consciousness any emotions that are inhibiting the natural flow of energy. By choosing to be nude and not receiving touch as opposed to partially clothed and receiving touch, one is empowering oneself and using their words and their consciousness to set boundaries rather than unconsciously relying on clothing.

This can be very powerful for women, many of whom have not had the experience of being naked with a man outside of a sexual situation. Getting comfortable with nudity is extremely important in healing our sexuality; otherwise nudity remains inextricably linked to sexuality in our minds. This may result in dissociative sexual behavior, which is linked to the desire for emotional release associated with nudity rather sexually arousal.

Another way to say this is that if you are comfortable being nude even in a mixed gender situation, you will not engage sexually just because you are aroused at the sight of nudity. For many people, the sight of a naked man may be deeply troubling because subconsciously we associate nudity with sexuality and sexuality with violence. And by maintaining the prohibition on nudity in most places and situations we create repression that, in turn, increases the likelihood of sexual violence and trauma.

The airbrushing ritual should be done first energetically and then skin to skin as lightly as possible. It is a simple matter to omit areas that the receiver has drawn boundary against being touched such as the genitals, buttocks, or breasts. Even if there are no boundaries, it is important to keep the touch in motion at all times and not focus on some areas of the body to the exclusion of others. You can vary the speed and move between light touch and no touch, but do not go into deeper touch or start to massage specific parts of the body. In this way, the whole body is energized, awakened, and expanded. Some people many experience full-body, non-ejaculatory orgasms, particularly if they are receiving from more than one person during this ritual.

Whole Body Touch Ritual

A more advanced exercise is to focus on the 3 aspects of touch (location, speed and pressure) and expand the location to the whole body excluding the genital region. This allows one to focus on practicing the skills of giving and receiving without needing to be concerned about genital contact. By explicitly agreeing to keep this area off-limits, one can focus on the present moment as opposed to thinking about what *may* happen.

This ritual can be very soothing, gentle and nurturing, or more stimulating, and may incorporate erotic energy. Ideally, the ritual will incorporate nurturing and relaxing as well as activating and energizing. This is an opportunity to explore the desires of both the giver and receiver and to communicate clearly. It is also a good way to practice moving beyond default patterns wherein we avoid asking for what we want, or block another by directing them when one is receiving. To help see if you have a clear default pattern here, ask yourself and then ask your friends and lovers if they see a clear pattern in you.

When touching the whole body it is good to ask a few basic questions such as:

1) Will you tell me if anything is painful or uncomfortable or if you want a pause or an end to the session?

2) Do you have an intention you would like to tell me or speak silently to yourself?

3) Do you have any injuries or sensitive areas of your body that I should be aware of or avoid?

4) Is there anything that is preventing you from being in the present moment with me right now?

These four basic questions should be enough to get accurate information for the giver to proceed. The will also reassure the receiver, allowing them to relax and receive more.

Start with grounding and relaxing touch. A good place to begin is at the feet just like with the power spot ritual. This enables the body to expand more during the activating phase of the ritual. And at the end it is best to come back again to grounding touch, ending with still touch that enables the experience to be integrated.

As the giver, allow yourself to touch in a way that is easeful and enjoyable for you. Don't try too hard to give pleasure; allow yourself to enjoy the giving. If you find you are getting aroused or distracted, slow your touch while you get centered and grounded. If you are getting sleepy or lethargic, move into more stimulating touch.

If you are the receiver, it's best to focus on yourself, closing your eyes and only opening them periodically or if asked to by the giver. Focus on deep slow breathing to help you relax and open to more sensation in your body. Once you are in a state of relaxation and feel grounded, you can allow your breath to move naturally, but remain focused on the breath without trying to control it.

It can be challenging for some people to receive without giving. This is another way our emotional body expands. By taking on different roles, by both giving and receiving, we learn about ourselves and others.

Chest, Heart and Breast Touch Ritual

Most massage therapists are trained to avoid women's breasts rather than simply asking if they would like to have them massaged. This takes the power of choice away from women and deprives them of experiencing nurturing breast touch, which is highly therapeutic and detoxifying.

It is recommended that women do self-examination of their breasts on a regular basis. Considering that breast cancer is a leading cause of death for middle-aged women, it is *imperative* that we demystify and encourage breast touch.

Just as with other questions, the giver can ask the receiver a few simple questions to ascertain the level of breast touch to which the receiver is open. And remember, the receiver can change her mind at any time.

Questions for Breast Touch:

Would you like me to put a stationary hand over your heart on your chest?
Would you like me to massage your breast excluding your nipples?
Would you like me to massage your whole breasts including your nipples?

The first stage of touch is a stationary hand over the heart or the center of the chest that can even be done without making contact but just holding a hand a few inches away. Or if desired, the hand can be placed with medium light stationary pressure over the center of the chest. Just holding a hand here, and perhaps the other hand behind the heart on the back, can be enough to encourage relaxation and major emotional releases.

The second stage of breast touch is to massage the breasts without contacting the nipple area, which is even more sensitive and erotically charged. One of the best strokes is to hold the arm over the head and massage down the arm, over the armpit and down the side of the breast towards the feet. This encourages lymphatic drainage, draining the lymph fluid from the lymph nodes in this region. This is where breast cancer often starts.

Lymphatic drainage strokes can come very close to the nipples without touching them or remain further away. Either way, by making a long, even stroke, the breast is connected and integrated with the rest of the body.

If the receiver desires more full breast touch including the nipples, you can then massage around the whole breast and the nipples. At first you may want to just slide over the nipples, which wakes up the nerve receptors and integrates the nipples with the breasts and the rest of the body. If desired, and you can trust this is the case if you have already asked the questions above, you can give special attention to the nipples by lightly grazing, then squeezing, rolling, and pulling the nipples. It is not unusual for this to build erotic energy, but for the purpose of breast massage, it is best not to act on it.

After doing breast and nipple massage for awhile, move away and towards another area of the body. This helps build trust and expand the range of sensation and response by building erotic energy without moving from the breasts to the genitals right away. One way to re-pattern sexuality is by changing the standard sequence of breast touch followed immediately by genital touch. It also allows for the energy generated in the breasts to be spread and integrated into the rest of the body.

Conscious Genital Touch

In sexual healing and empowerment sessions we incorporate genital touch if, and only if, the receiver explicitly asks for that. I just simply state at the beginning of a session with a woman that I am not going to touch her yoni unless I feel she is present, ready and able to integrate yoni touch and she explicitly asks for it. A conscious genital massage is very useful to open up sexually because it gives full attention to the sensations in the genitals and the rest of the body without the receiver having to do anything or reciprocate. This, simply put, is the great benefit of the practice: to simply relax, receive, and enjoy genital touch. Most of the time we are receiving and giving at the same time whej sexing with a partner. Or we are masturbating and fantasizing. And we are usually working energetically to create more sexual energy, to create more connection, to have an orgasm, to give an orgasm, to find release.

Conscious genital touch is a way of re-patterning that sexual conditioning and releasing us from goal-oriented sexual behavior. We can just lie down and be touched without needing to do anything else. That is very relaxing, though it can be very challenging to someone whose pattern is to give or who has fear in receiving from another.

My sexual healing and empowerment sessions that incorporate genital touch last a minimum of 2 hours although they may go 3 or 4 hours. Often women put up sexual blocks, even when they want sexual connection, because they have had experience with men pushing for more in the past, or pushing beyond their sexual boundaries, which may or may not have been expressed. In a conscious genital touch practice we make an explicit agreement **not** to have sex during or immediately after the practice. Let me say that again, the conscious genital touch practice is not a form of foreplay or prelude to sexual intercourse. It is whole and complete unto itself. Of course, with a lover, it is a wonderful practice that may lead to lovemaking. But it is important for the receiver to know there is no expectation of other sexual interactions and that the touch being given is given as a gift, not an attempt to engage in sexual activity. This allows women to relax deeply relax, and helps a man focus on what is in front of him rather than on his arousal. Often men are so goal oriented they spend an entire lovemaking session striving for orgasm and fail to appreciate what is occurring in the rest of the body, in their emotions and their mind.

This is a time to slow down, breathe, open and connect with oneself without any goal. This is a meditative practice. Just like sitting in meditation, a non-sexual form of meditation can greatly increase our consciousness by allowing us to watch the mind.

This act of witnessing, or mindfulness, cultivates sensitivity that is an important part of building connection with others and ourselves. To be sensitive to our bodies and our emotions is to increase self-knowledge. And that allows us to know others more deeply. We can only be as perceptive with another as we are with ourselves. This is why the practice is so simple and why it differs from many other tantric sexual practices. It is not so much a technique, but a practice of mindful attention.

Painful and legal or Pleasurable and illegal?

When another person touches our genitals or in the genital area of the body it is most often with the goal of sexual stimulation. Or if a person without that goal does it, they often treat the genitals roughly or without sensitivity such as in gynecological or prostate exams. In fact, in many places it is illegal to touch a person's genitals in a professional encounter (i.e. where money is exchanged) if the touch is pleasurable. Women who receive a Brazilian bikini wax are paying for a session where their labia are touched and stripped of hair. This is legal because it is not pleasurable. And men can receive a prostate exam or a penis piercing by a tattoo artist legally as long as there is no pleasure. What more proof do you need of a pleasure-negative society?

Of course, these laws are changing. In California it is possible to be legally sanctioned as a sexological bodyworker and in more advanced countries such as parts of Europe, Australia, New Zealand, and Canada, professional pleasurable genital touch is legal.

Pelvic Release

When I do sessions, I am not only massaging slowly but also deeply, connecting with the bones and joints in the pelvic region. This type of massage is so different from a sexual touching, the client can go into a relaxed healing mode. Sessions often last over 2 hours, with a full hour devoted to massaging and opening the pelvic area.

The pelvic release work can also be done without contacting the genitals either internally or externally. Massaging the pelvic area is often omitted or given light or cursory strokes in a typical therapeutic massage. By focusing on massaging the pelvic area in a non-sexual way, we can release stored tensions and emotions that are tied to this area. The key is going even slower with more sensitivity and grounding pressure than normally in a massage.

Pelvic massage should be done <u>prior</u> to any genital contact as it is very important to help the pelvic area unwind before any genital stimulation. And by stating clearly that I won't be touching the genitals unless asked by the receiver, I can work very closely to the genitals unlike in most massage sessions. Many of the techniques I use in pelvic release work come from traditional Thai massage and are very effective in opening the joints in the body. Because of this, it can be best to work on a mat rather than a massage table. If you are planning to incorporate genital touch in your healing work, I strongly suggest you learn pelvic release techniques in traditional Thai massage. Rather than go into all the moves here, if you are interested to learn this in an in-depth manner you can take a Thai massage training course and/or read books on Thai massage.

The main difference between how I work and traditional Thai massage is that I usually work with the client disrobed and use oil whereas in Thai massage the client is fully clothed and no oil is used. By integrating Thai massage with Lomi-Lomi, I combine strong yang or masculine energy with a more fluid, yin or feminine approach synthesizing the best of both to deeply relax, open and tonify the body while increasing awareness and encouraging emotional release.

I will do pelvic release work with the receiver clothed and, when they are ready, encourage them to receive without clothing. This enables them to experience a deep level of relaxation while disrobed that is key to anchoring in the parasympathetic nervous system during sex.

Hand and Body Positions for Genital Touch Sessions

To give a woman a conscious genital massage, invite her to lie down on her back on a yoga mat or on a very firm blanket or mattress on the floor. I do not recommend practicing at first on a bed because beds are usually not firm enough and the fact that people usually have sex in beds can distract from the intention of sexual re-patterning.

The main position I use in sessions is to be seated between her legs, best with a firm pillow under my butt so my hips are elevated. In this position, with a firm pillow or meditation cushion called a zafu, I can sit for hours without getting a sore back. This is important because anything that creates discomfort for you will distract and desensitize you to what the receiver is feeling and experiencing.

This position is the best in my estimation for mapping and emotional release work where other positions may be better suited to more energetic activating touch. Another advantage of the parallel-between-the-legs-position is it gives you the option of supporting the receiver's back and chest with your feet if you are flexible enough to do it. While it may seem initially strange, placing your feet under her back will elevate the chest and open the throat. This is helpful in opening the spine and allowing the energy to move up and out. Many women who have been abused or assaulted have difficulty in speaking up and have a block in their throats energetically. This position will encourage deep breathing and making sound, which may help release emotions.

In the second position, you can approach her perpendicularly, coming in from her side. Sit on a meditation cushion or several firm pillows to elevate your hips. Put one leg over her abdominal area and one leg under her knees and thighs. To help her be more comfortable and fully relax, put another pillow under her knee that is farther away from you.

In this position you should both be fully relaxed and comfortable. Take a few deep breaths and adjust your body if necessary to reach alignment and comfort. Whatever your position, it's good to take time to get comfortable and to switch positions if you are getting stiff in one position. A daily yoga practice is extremely helpful in this regard.

In the perpendicular position, you have more options for hand positions that I will discuss more in the upcoming section on activation and expansion.

After we have done the initial intake, the emotional release and communication work, the whole body touch and the pelvic release work, she is ready for genital contact if she desires it. Here it is important to pause, and for her to re-focus on what is in her field of awareness. What are you aware of at the level of sensation in your body? What emotions are you aware of right now? Are you having any thoughts, memories or fantasies?

If I sense there is anything present that is unexpressed I'll ask about it before any genital contact as the goal is to be as present as possible so the experience can shift old patterns as much as possible.

When I do make contact, I will bring my hand down to rest with the weight of gravity, gently but firmly cupping her whole yoni. Pausing, breathing, eye-gazing at this deeper level of physical intimacy is crucial to building trust and helping her to access any stored emotions. Sometimes women start to cry at this point, which signals an emotional release. Just as with any other emotional release, it is best to just continue the physical contact without movement, holding space for the release to occur fully. If I sense the experience may be too intense, I may ask if she wants me to move my hand away from her yoni. Even during really intense emotional releases, the woman almost always wants me to keep my hand cupping and holding her yoni.

Exterior Yoni massage

After making the initial contact I usually start to massage the pubic mound and then the outer labia. Massaging slowly from the outside towards the midline and opening of the vagina, I take plenty of time to massage up and down, focusing on making contact with every area repeatedly and connecting all the areas together in long slow strokes. I also let her know that I will not enter her unless she explicitly asks me to and I sense she is ready and able to integrate internal yoni massage. Levels of physical intimacy here are: bringing the hand close to but not touching her yoni, cupping her yoni, pubic mound massage, outer labia, inner labia, clitoris, and introitus (the opening of the vagina).

While I am massaging her yoni I look at her face and her eyes and notice her breathing. I will check in every once in a while and ask, "Does that feel good?" or another simple question that can be answered with a "yes" or a "no". If I sense she is dissociating, I will pause and ask her what is in her field of awareness. If she doesn't answer or open her eyes, I will make light contact with her third eye point between her eyebrows.

Even if a woman seems to be very relaxed and enjoying the massage she could still be dissociating so it is crucial that we pause, make eye contact and have at least some verbal connection at different times throughout the session.

Connecting with the Clitoris

After I have massaged the pubic mound and the outer and inner labia, I will usually move on to the clitoris. This bundle of nerves and tissues comes to head above the introitus or opening of the vagina. Some women have a pronounced clitoral hood that obscures the clitoris entirely; on other women the hood barely covers the clitoris. It is important to note that the clitoral nerves extend from the clitoris down either side of yoni, beneath the labia. This means that when we are massaging up and down the labia we are starting to make contact with the clitoris and this prepares the clitoris for more direct contact.

In general I find it best to make contact with and massage over the hood of the clit first before pulling the hood back and making directly contact with the clitoris. It's important to note that if she has a pronounced clitoral hood that completely covers the clitoris, you may have difficulty pulling the hood back if you have used too much lube.

The point of massaging the clitoris here is not stimulation or orgasm but to connect it with the rest of the yoni and to use the energy generated to make increase her desire for internal yoni touch. Some people perform yoni massage or sexual healing sessions without focusing much on the clitoris because it can be very arousing and distract from the other parts of the body and the yoni. My usual approach is to contact the clitoris but not to give it too much attention, just enough attention to put energy in the system without distracting from everything else that is occurring. So throughout the yoni massage, I'll often keep a rhythm going on the clitoris with one finger while focusing more on the internal mapping and releasing discussed below.

Pulsing the Introitus

Before entering the inside of the yoni, it's useful to pay attention to the gatekeeper of the yoni, the introitus. This area is often overlooked in the hurry to penetrate the vagina. If the woman is not sufficiently aroused and lubricated, this area can be stressed or even torn in the mad rush to get inside. There are a lot of nerves in this area and massaging it can be very pleasurable.

The introitus also serves as the "pause point" before entering the vagina. If I sense a woman would like to be entered I will pause at the introitus and sense if she is ready or not. As further preparation for penetration, I will often linger at the introitus and pulse it rhythmically for some time, sending waves of energy throughout the yoni and creating a suction pull that activates the inner walls of the vagina. I usually use a thumb and without going inside, I move my thumb up and down, creating the waves and the suction pressure.

Re-framing Penetration as Envelopment

Before entering the vagina I usually suggest the woman consciously focus her attention on her yoni and use her muscles to pull or suck me inside. While many women are not experienced in using these muscles in this way, it is extremely useful to bring their awareness to this innate ability and encourage them to practice envelopment. Besides building a better connection between the yoni, nerve and muscle tissues, mind and body, this exercise is very empowering as I encourage them to decide exactly when and who they invite inside their body.

By describing it as envelopment rather than penetration, women are seen as active rather than passive participants in a sexual encounter. For far too long, women have been passive recipients of male sexuality. Simply using this word envelopment can alter a woman's perception and give her a greater sense of her power and choice.

To increase her ability to envelope, women should get a jade egg or similar egg shaped stone that they can practice moving up and down inside their vaginas. The egg can have a hole drilled in it so a string can be attached and the egg removed if she can't push it out.

Eggs are available in the better sensual boutiques and in many online stores. Good descriptions of the use of jade eggs are found in Mantak Chia's books on Taoist sexuality.

Clock Exercise

One way to help a receiver connect more deeply to their genitals and help them release body armor and emotions is the clock exercise. After you have massaged the exterior areas of the genital region, you can ask the receiver if they want to receive internal massage and mapping. Some practitioners de-eroticize this work to the point that they discourage any stimulation of the genitals first. If the receiver wants this type of session, fine. But there is value in leaving it up to the individual whether they want to receive pleasure during the session or not. Pleasure is a great lubricant. And when someone is sexually excited they open up more, both physically and emotionally. And our sensitivity to our own body increases as long as we stay connected and grounded. If a major part of the reason for doing a session is to help a receiver feel more pleasure, why would we intentionally move away from giving them pleasure?

After doing some external genital massage, I like to do internal mapping. Basically the mapping process in the clock exercise is to imagine the internal points as corresponding to positions on a clock, with 12 "hours" or 12 different locations around the circular interior area. For a more precise mapping, you can add 3 depths: shallow, medium and deep.

If you are working with a woman I suggest starting at 12 o'clock, which corresponds to the anterior (towards her belly), and moving around the vagina from 1-6 o'clock (6 o'clock is towards the perineum and anus) and back up to 12 o'clock. It is good to keep steady pressure at each point but not push too hard on the G-spot (at 12 o'clock) as this is a highly sensitive zone and can be painful for some women. A specific G-spot or sacred spot massage can be done later after the mapping process is concluded or in another session. If too much stimulation is given to the G-spot, the sensations and emotions can be so intense that the receiver may have less awareness of the other locations of the yoni or become focused on orgasm.

Going around the clock, tell the receiver where you are, such as: "Now we are at 3 o'clock (towards their left leg) with medium depth. What sensations and emotions are you experiencing?" If they are experiencing little or no sensation, introduce a little rhythmic movement. If they are experiencing strong emotions, continue to hold the point, encourage them to breathe deeply and express what . Remind them you can stop at any point: most people will want to continue.

If you are going slowly and mapping each point along the 3 depths, this process alone can take between 1-2 hours. Give yourself time to really dive in and make sure you are in a comfortable position so as to avoid straining your body. If you are sitting on your butt in the perpendicular position I recommend, make sure your hips are elevated to avoid back strain. Any strain in your body will be an impediment to sensing your receiver and allowing them to releas tension and emotions.

De-armoring the cervix

If possible, it is best to make contact with and map the cervix and the areas around it as well. If it is possible to go this deeply inside it is good to do so to provide an opportunity to release any emotion stored in this area. The cervix may be numb or tender/painful to the touch. Often there is not much sensation at first because many women have been conditioned to allow sex when they are not ready or allow sex that is faster, harder, and deeper than is pleasurable.

Because the vast majority of men get their primary sex education from explicit videos that promote fast, hard sex, women are often subject to this type of sex, which can be very damaging to the cervical area. Once a woman is fully aroused, her cervix retracts to allow more space for the lingam to move inside her. If she is not aroused and her cervix is continually hit forcefully, her cervix will become armored and even numb. Unfortunately, this is the case for many women and until they have a conscious genital massage, they may not realize how much trauma is held in their cervix and yoni.

When you make contact with the cervix, understand that this is a very tight bundle of tissue that separates the vagina from the uterus. This is the sacred place where babies emerge from the womb. Treat it with the utmost respect and sensitivity. The cervix is also capable of a powerful orgasm that dwarfs the clitoral orgasm by comparison. It is extremely deep and literally the invitation for a man's seed to enter and start a new life.

When I make contact with the cervix, I ask if she can feel any sensations, emotions or memories related to this area. I keep a finger with constant pressure on the head of the cervix and then map around the head of the cervix and behind it. I go very slowly and may even place the cervix between two fingers to help her connect and feel it more accurately.

The emphasis here is on re-connecting conscious awareness to this part of the body. When an area of the body is numb, the electrical impulses from the nerves are not consciously received by the brain. To bring back sensation, awareness and pleasure, we need to connect the numb areas with areas where there is awareness of sensation. This requires going slowly and communicating exactly what we are doing and where we are touching. Creating a mental picture for the woman is very useful in helping her to regain awareness and sensitivity.

When having intercourse with a lover, I attune to the cervix and set an intention to massage the cervix with my lingam. There is a position that is very well suited to this type of cervical massage with the woman on her belly with the man sitting on top of her with his knees on either side of her buttocks. In this position I can easily rock my pelvis back and forth, which massages all the way from the front to the back of her cervix with both the front and back of the head of my lingam. Another good position is yab-yum position with the woman sitting with legs wrapped around the seated man. In this position the man should hold the woman tightly and firmly press his lingam around the cervix without drawing the lingam in and out of her.

These positions and movements are very useful because the cervix has often become armored due to unconscious thrusting, penetrating too fast, too deeply, or before the woman is ready. Women enjoy very deep penetration when they are ready, but to get to this level of penetration often requires and hour or more of lovemaking. This requires communication and grounding, as well as ejaculation control on the man's part. A woman will unconsciously "milk" a man's penis if she is in fear or if she is addicted to sharp peak orgasms.

Reclaiming the G-spot

For a long time the G-spot was debated, denied and even ridiculed. Now it is accepted as fact and focused on, often to the exclusion of other areas of a woman's yoni and body. Far too often, both men and women focus on the G-spot as merely a pleasure button, pushing it as hard and fast as possible.

While the G-spot can be very pleasurable, it also can be desensitized in women who are not as aware or empowered in their sexuality. It is another tight bundle of tissue that tends to hold memories and emotional charges. So it is crucial that we first make contact with the G-spot with a focus on healing and releasing any energy it is holding.

If you have performed pelvic release work, external yoni massage, internal mapping such as the clock exercise, you are ready to make contact with the G-spot. I suggest doing any cervical touch <u>before</u> G-spot work as you may move from G-spot mapping and releasing into activating the G-spot. It is best to do all mapping and releasing work <u>before</u> moving into activation and expansion of pleasure. Otherwise the mapping and releasing may not happen and areas of numbness, pain or stuck emotions may not be found and released.

The G-spot is another area that often is armored due to trauma resulting in a lack of sensitivity and awareness. The urethral sponge that makes up the G-spot is located on the anterior (belly side) wall of the vagina, a couple inches inside. To find it, curl one finger towards the belly and inside 2 inches or so. Its location varies from woman to woman, but it should feel firm with ridges that are distinct from the surrounding tissue Just as with cervical mapping and releasing, it is good to make contact with the whole area, feeling if there are areas of numbness, pain, or stored emotions. Take your time and really feel this area instead of just rubbing it as hard and fast as you can.

Many people are fixated on G-spot orgasms and on ejaculation. These naturally occur with stimulation but should not be focused on as a goal. A woman can have an ejaculatory G-spot orgasm and still have a de-sensitized yoni, unreleased emotional material, and a tendency to dissociate. A G-spot orgasm and ejaculation are often looked at as "proof" that she is sexually whole.

Pelvic release and the various aspects of genital massage discussed above could take from several hours to several sessions depending on the history, personality and issues of different women. For some women, it is best to have several sessions of talking before any physical touch occurs and another several sessions of physical touch before genital touch occurs. By our presence, awareness and ability to discern where someone is emotionally, physically and psychologically, we can guide a woman through challenging terrain and help her to reach a state of ease, confidence and groundedness. By going slow we do not "heal" her but give her reference points for what she feels like when she is connected with herself. By encouraging her to speak her truth, to speak her sensations, emotions, thoughts and memories, we support her in her empowerment. While we are not engaged in a romantic relationship, we model healthy relating and respect. This way when she is in a relationship that is not serving her or healthy for her, she can tell the difference and will be less likely to remain stuck in those patterns and relationships.

Activation and Expansion

After contacting, massaging, mapping, and releasing points in and around the yoni, you may be ready for touch and other activities that are focused on activation and expansion of the range of sensation and emotion. But unless you have done the preliminary work, you run the risk of dissociative behavior and experiences that further compound pre-existing issues. Even if a man is very sensitive and loving, his actions may not be absorbed and integrated if she is unaware and still trying to find release from old hurts, traumas and patterns.

Only when she is in the present moment, aware of her body, her emotions and her desires, is she ready for activation and expansion. When we talk about activation and expansion, we are talking about ways to increase the range of sensation and emotion without dissociating. Dissociating is simply when we have experiences we can't integrate and thus go unconscious to one degree or another.

When we have the tools and empowerment to communicate clearly and authentically, we can go on a journey of expansion together. It is good to take a minute to close your eyes and connect with yourself at this point, and then when you feel grounded and centered you can start to touch the receiver with your hands.

It is useful to massage other parts of the body first before getting into this position, ideally at least 30-60 minutes of whole body touch. Remember, this should be done with the intention of relaxing and grounding, not with the intention of turning them, or yourself, on.

Once you feel that you and the receiver are sufficiently grounded you can move toward the genital stroking. If you are going to use gloves this is the time to put them on (nitrile non-latex gloves are better for people with a latex allergy). Announce when you are about to touch the genital area to make sure the recipient is ready to receive. You can say: "Would you like me to touch your yoni?" Or words that resonate for you and your partner.

It is best to pause, make eye contact, breath deeply, and tune in to make sure she is present and 100% sure of her choice to receive at this time. If she is, then take your hand and place it on her yoni, cupping over top of it and letting your hand rest just as you did in the power spot exercise. Pausing once you've made contact is important as we go deeper at each level of physical intimacy. It's good to ask now and again: "How's that feel?" or, "What's in your field of awareness right now?" If someone cannot answer, they are likely dissociating and you should not go into a deeper level of physical intimacy. If they are dissociating, you should encourage them to at least make sound if not words, to release whatever they are experiencing right now.

For activation and expansion, I often sit in the perpendicular position with one leg over her belly and one leg under her legs. I like to stroke with my right index finger and I use my left index finger, middle finger, and ring finger so I put lube on these fingers as well. I am careful not to put lube on my thumbs so I can spread her lips and pull the clitoral hood up to better stroke the clit. Some women have much more pronounced clitoral hoods so if she enjoys direct clitoral touch, you may have to pull and hold the clitoral hood back.

I position my hand so I can use my left index and middle fingers inside her vagina and even my ring finger inside her anus if desired.

In this position, I can stimulate her clitorally, vaginally with G-spot and cervical contact and anally all at the same time. Most of the time though, I stroke the clit with grounding pressure on the other areas. Remember, the goal is not maximum stimulation but maximum sensitivity and attention.

Especially in the beginning of a session or when you first start practicing, it is good not to focus on the internal spots. It may take several sessions for her to open to the point where she desires any strong, internal pressure. Just leave your fingers outside her until she is 100% ready and wanting them inside her. Tell her you will not enter her unless she asks.

You can give good grounding pressure by pushing down on the base of the introitus or opening of the vagina with your thumb. This is a good position for giving grounding pressure, but is does not allow use of the rest of the hand for internal pressure and stimulation, nor does it allow the thumb to be used to pull the hood of the clit back.

In the beginning of your practice keep it simple and just do whatever hand position seems comfortable for you.

Once you have your hands in position, you should start slowly, very slowly. Remember when you are being massaged you can feel everything more sensitively. You want to start very slowly and gently,which enables the receiver to trust, relax and open more fully to the experience. Spread some lube on the inside of the lips on the way up to the clit, then pull back the hood and hold light pressure on the clit before stroking.

Even this will be too much for some women. T he clit may be too sensitive for direct contact, so do more indirect strokes at first. C heck in with your partner and ask them "How's the stroke?" This gives them the opportunity to give you feedback and request a refinement in the stroking.

Practicing communicating while stroking and being stroked is another major benefit of the practice. Here is an opportunity to ask for what we want, to practice requesting in a clear, uncharged manner. "I'd like you to stroke more slowly," "Please stroke more lightly," "A little more to the left." This is very empowering and can be difficult for many who have not practiced verbal communication during sex.

It is a good spot to get to know, to explore and develop, yet I have found that exclusively focusing on that spot can concentrate energy there and be ungrounding. The primary focus was on woman's orgasm and the main route to reach that was the upper left quadrant of her clitoris.

I found that to assimilate and integrate my sexual energy I needed to do yoga, give and receive non-sexual massage and touch, be in nature, meditate, prepare food, and other activities. I find that I could only expand and reach heights of sensation and awareness when I am firmly grounded. .

Three Main Aspects in Genital Touch

The three main aspects of conscious genital massage are the same as for the rest of the body: speed, pressure, and location. By focusing on each aspect separately we increase our ability to give pleasure to our partner. Have you ever attempted to pat your head with an up and down motion with one hand and rub your belly in a circular direction with the other hand? Increasing our ability to do opposite movements with opposite hands is a skill that is very important for activities such as music or sports. And in sex, developing subtle skills make the difference between a good lover and an exceptional one. Of course there is much more to being a good lover than just technique, but if you want to really please your lover, it is worth practicing just as you might practice playing an instrument.

The process of developing your skills is not so much a practice of doing something to get a specific result. The key is to attune ourselves to the other person and develop our intuition so we can give them the most pleasurable touch possible. Doing this without attachment to the effect is important to staying present. If you are focused on giving your partner an orgasm, you may miss opportunities to experience many other pleasurable states. Again, this is why it is so important to clear the emotional body before engaging sexually rather than using orgasm as an emotional release technique.

Speed

You would think by now that every sexually active heterosexual man would know that women do not appreciate being touched as fast as possible. Stroking rapidly has its place, but far too often, men engage in fast stroking when they are excited and as a compensation for their performance insecurity and lack of creativity. Try stroking as slow as possible. At least in the beginning of a session or a sexual experience it is almost always better to start slowly. This conveys confidence to a woman and women respond to confidence. Once you are in a nice rhythm you can increase the tempo, sustain it for a while and then drop down to a slower pace rather than just increasing the speed to the goal of orgasm. This is important in developing an awareness of peaks and valleys. After a while, you may experience a valley orgasm, an orgasm of a noticeably different variety than a sharp peak. Just as slower, deeper breathing has a noticeable relaxing and grounding effect on consciousness, slower stroking can have a similar effect.

Pressure

Similarly, many men have been conditioned to stroke too hard with too much pressure. You can learn a lot about how a man will stroke you if you watch him masturbate. Most men are conditioned to masturbate with a fast, hard stroke to maximize stimulation and reach orgasm and ejaculation as quickly as possible. Men who masturbate in this manner will likely stroke their partners in a similar fashion. It is the ego that wants a response and many men can be a bully when it comes to touching their partner's genitals. Try stroking as lightly as possible, so lightly that you can barely tell you are touching. It is important to note that pressure and speed are different aspects and you can have four different approaches just in regard to speed and pressure. You can stroke slowly and lightly, slowly and firmly, fast and firm or fast and light. When in doubt, stroke more lightly. To expand and open, most women want less pressure.

Location

As with pressure and speed, there are myriad locations for stroking. The clitoris may resemble an "on" button to you and even to her, but there is far more than the clitoris that is deserving of attention.

I suggest starting entirely outside the pelvic region and gradually warming up the whole body through progressively deeper grounding pressure and strokes. Once you get to the lips of the yoni, you will have warmed up the tissue and prepared the receiver for some time. It is useful to contact much, if not all of the genital area before the clitoris is contacted and certainly before any penetration begins.

So many different areas exist outside of the yoni: the outer lips, the inner lips the valley between the inner and outer lips, the bottom of the introitus or opening to the vagina, the mons above the pubic bone and above the clitoris. Take time and try out a variety of speeds and pressures at different locations.

What type of stroke do you favor? A utilitarian up down/up down stroke? A circling, curving, spiraling meander? A seductive curling come-hither stroke? A jazzy, sideway angular shot? There are probably as many varieties of strokes as there are people. Unfortunately, lack of self-confidence, lack of curious exploration and many centuries of shame have limited our range of possibilities when it comes to sexual touch. As much as variety is important and exciting, it is useful to drop into the rhythm of a particular stroke and stay with it. There is a reason women go nuts for musicians; if a man can keep a beat and stay grounded while demonstrating creativity and dexterity with an instrument, he will likely be a good lover, or so the assumption goes. And it is probably a good assumption given the success of musicians with women.

Once you have a good stroke that feels good to you and your partner, keep going and get into the rhythm of it. I suggest that you stay focused and attentive to your partner *and* at the same time, stroke in a manner that resonates with your desire and sensations. How much sensation are you capable of in your finger?

To orgasm or not?

People often ask, "Should I orgasm during a genital massage session." Generally I recommend riding the peaks and valleys of sensation instead of going over the edge. It's not wrong to go over the edge, but you do miss the opportunity to expand your orgasm rather than go for a quick release.

This is part of the reason why we practice the conscious emotional release process *before* a genital massage session. We want to clear the emotional body first, so we can connect with sensation directly and not use genital massage as an opportunity for emotional release. Emotional release may come as a result, but it is best to clear all the emotional charges we have before we start to stroke. Then if we have an emotional release, we are likely to have a deeper release coming from a deeper, more subconscious level of our being.

And by doing the emotional release work first, the giver is more able to be centered and grounded and able to hold space for an emotional release. This is why it is so crucial not to be focused on a sharp peak of orgasm or release, but to allow space for releases to happen naturally.

When finished stroking, give the receiver holding pressure, sometimes very firm pressure, on the introitus, the pubic bone and elsewhere in the pelvic region such as the hips. Women often want a surprising amount of pressure; inversely proportional to how lightly they may want to be stroked. This grounding pressure is a time for integration and assimilation of the sensations that were just experienced.

The Importance of Meditation and Eye-gazing

After a session it is very useful to sit in silent meditation so each person can return to center and reconnect with themselves without focusing on their partner. At the beginning of a session or lovemaking, meditation helps us come into the present moment, to become more aware of our breath, our body, our emotions and to become more present for our partner so we can attune to them. By silently meditating and then opening your eyes when you are ready for engagement with your partner you create a powerful ritual that, when repeated over time, creates resonance with your partner. Silently eye-gazing with your partner allows time for your breath to synchronize with each other. Notice any sensations, emotions, thoughts or perceptions that arise while you gaze.

If an emotion, sensation or thought, emerges strongly in your field of awareness you can share it with your partner using the communication rituals you have practiced. You can share a revelation or give a perception at this time; this can create more trust and understanding so you can drop into a deeper space of intimacy.

Resistance

Resistance is when someone is pulling back, pushing away, or denying something they desire. We experience resistance when we have a blockage that prevents us from getting what we want. Just as in an electrical system, resistance generates heat. People are usually unconscious of their patterns of resistance. Once they become aware, they can either choose what is being offered and accept it, or reject it. We are in resistance when we blocking something or someone, but refuse to let go.

A key part of doing conscious sensuality work is in generating awareness of and dissolving resistance. This is not to say that we just open ourselves to anything and anyone, but to connect with our desire so we can actively receive and trust our desires. When we do not trust our desires, we manufacture a blockage to protect us. This causes resistance. When we are fully empowered and trust ourselves to follow desire, we have far more vital energy because we are not expending energy creating blockages and maintaining resistance. Fear pushing against desire is resistance.

Zen Sex and going slow

"In the beginners mind there are many possibilities" – Zen Mind, Beginners Mind by Shunryu Suzuki

This is a good exercise for undoing patterns of force and speed. Get into position with your partner and begin to touch extremely slowly. See how slowly you can touch while moving your finger. It helps to have really good lube. Imagine you are a tiny insect walking your way up the clitoris. When you reach the ridge of the bottom of the hood of the clit start again. Very slowly up and down along the clit. Notice what sensations are arising in your body. Are you tense? Contracted? Holding your breath? Do you notice sensations in your finger? Elsewhere in your body?

When you desire it, increase your speed, but increase it very slowly. Rather than shifting gears on a car, increase the speed as slowly as you can. After a while, slow down again. Notice what sensations this brings up.

You can do this internally as well if this is desired by both of you. Stroke the G-spot very softly and slowly. At what point can the receiver sense the motion? Curl your finger rather than just pulling out and pushing in. Curl your finger very slowly from the back of the vagina towards the front. Feel every ridge and valley of the G-spot. You can alternate the speed and pressure then go back to a very slow and gentle stroke.

Experiment by alternating between light, quick strokes and firm, slow strokes. The more we practice different ways of touching, the more our ability to connect increases, and the more sensitive we become.

This practice is akin to a pianist doing the musical scales. It builds skill that makes them more adept when they play a song. Rather than rigidly doing the practice again and again as if by rote, bring a fresh consciousness to the practice every time. This opens more possibilities and avenues for exploration.

In this type of sex, we use the will and intention to clear the mind so we can see more clearly. It is a fundamentally different approach than tantric practices that use tools such as visualization, yantra, and elaborate rituals to bring the practitioner to a state of awareness. A Zen approach to sexuality is to watch desire, sensation and emotion without manipulating it for a specific goal. Rather than to use the sexual experience as strategy for enlightenment, Zen sex is enlightenment.

Re-Patterning Masturbation As Self-Pleasure

Our ability to give loving touch and presence to another is directly related to our ability to give loving touch to ourselves. Too often we ignore our own needs and focus on pleasing others, subconsciously making them responsible for meeting our own needs. Masturbation is often done as quickly as possible to reach the goal of physical and emotional release.

Masturbation can be very useful to help us see ourselves and release our patterns. An unconscious, unloving, release-focused practice can end up distancing us from others. But when we reclaim our right to self-pleasure and practice it with mindfulness, it can have great benefits.

One of the benefits of conscious self-pleasure is insight into what turns us on. The vast majority of men masturbate to visual stimulation, either explicit videos or pictures, or fantasy images in their minds. In pursuit of their goal of release, they are often unaware of their breath ignorant as to the power of emotions, and oblivious to their sensations.

When we take time to release our emotions regularly, exercise, stretch and get massage, we can take more time with our self-pleasure practice as we are not in need of using masturbation for these purposes. And when we take time, slow down and breathe, we can turn masturbation into a meditation.

Breathing slowly and consciously as we touch ourselves, we can focus on sensations in our bodies and gain awareness of our emotions and thoughts.

Who or what do you think of as you masturbate? Is it someone you know? A movie star? A porn star? Someone you recently met? What is the fantasy you have with this person? Can you empty your mind completely and let go of all fantasies and be turned on by yourself? Can you enjoy sensations without stimulating thoughts?

Do you touch other parts of your body besides your sexual organs? How about your nipples? Your lips? Your hair? Do you associate loving yourself in this way with homosexuality? Would you be comfortable pleasuring yourself in this way in front of another person? In the presence of your lover? What fears or judgments come up as you imagine masturbating in front of different people?

Doing a self-pleasure ritual with a group is an advanced practice. It is crucial that everyone is truly focused on themselves and not just harvesting energy from watching others touch themselves. To get to a place where people can do this, it is important that the ritual be held in a space of love, trust and awareness. To do this, approached it just as you do other rituals, focusing on individual meditation and self-awareness first.

Once people are grounded and connected to themselves, they can relax and begin to really feel themselves through their own touch. Touching your own body from head to toe over an extended period of time, at least 30 minutes, before touching your genitals is a powerful way to re-pattern your masturbation practice as a self-pleasure practice.

An additional support for this practice is in choosing music that cultivates a state of relaxation and awareness. For my self-pleasure audio cd, I decided to work with a leader in the field of sound healing, Ashera Hart. Ashera is an expert on the sounds that support greater consciousness. For our audio recording, we used the Solfeggio frequencies, which are specifically calibrated to have maximum effect on the brain and create a theta brain wave state.

Anal and Prostate Pleasure

One of the best ways for a man to be introduced to anal and prostate pleasure is through his self-pleasure practice. If a man has little experience with anal pleasure, he can explore this area of his body all by himself with no need to pay attention to anyone else.

Stroking the penis while fingering the anus is not only pleasurable but a powerful way to boost energy and increase capacity for sensation. For me, being pleasured anally allows me to experience a much greater level of sensation in my penis without ejaculating. I have experienced so much sensation throughout my body at times, that it was comparable to an out-of-body-experience. A good book on this subject is Anal Pleasure and Health by the late Jack Morin.

Expanding your range of sensation and emotion though anal touch is important. Often strong emotions and traumas can be hidden or stored in this part of the body. Often people carry a lot of shame in this area and re-connecting it to pleasure is crucial to our sexual health and power.

For men, receiving prostate massage is vital to health and prevention of cancer. It also greatly helps men to understand what it is like to be penetrated, which increases their sensitivity when penetrating their partner.

Self-Pleasuring Ritual

Give yourself at least ½ hour or more for this ritual. I like to do this once a week on the day off from my yoga practice. The idea is to massage ourselves all over our bodies and to give ourselves the touch we would like to receive from another person. Especially for men, this can be a difficult exercise. Many have internalized the messages that to suffer and be in pain and discomfort is part of their lot in life and their identity as a man. And though women are culturally sanctioned to nurture themselves more, all the beautification, pampering, spa treatments, etc. is often part of a strategy to please men and society, rather than for self-care or self-love purposes.

Start with a prayer, an intention and some deep breathing to center yourself. Turn on some slow meditative music that will help you relax and go slowly. Create the space around you to reflect how you would like it to be for a very special date. In this case, the date is with yourself.

Begin touching yourself by contacting your heart with one or both hands firmly but gently on your chest. Then move from the center of the chest out to the shoulder and one of your arms. Massage the shoulder fully and work your way down your arm to your other hand. Use a good massage oil such as almond or coconut oil. Using oil helps to warm up and loosen the body; it increases fluidity in the strokes, which encourages relaxation. Now do the other arm starting at the shoulder.

From the arms you can massage your head, face and neck. Give loving attention to areas such as your eyes and ears. Try pulling, twisting and gently touching your ears; encouraging them to release stored tension.

Move down your neck onto your chest and give yourself firm massage, stretching the powerful muscles in your chest. If you want you can give special attention to your nipples, generating more erotic energy in your system. Now move towards your belly and massage your stomach and other internal organs. Move your hands in the direction of digestion from the right to the left side of your belly and down towards the pelvic region.

Now massage your lower back, contacting the sacrum and your kidneys. Moving down, massage your buttocks and then down each of your legs towards your feet. Give special attention to your feet. You can spend a long time massaging someone else's feet, why not your own?

Having given loving attention to every area of your body except your genitals now you are ready to give them some attention as well. Maintain the same loving attention and touch that you just gave to the rest of your body. See if you can massage yourself in a slow, pleasurable way without needing to orgasm or ejaculate. See if you can be present to the sensation in your body without going into fantasy.

When you feel complete, whether you have had an orgasm or not, return to a place of stillness with a hand on the heart and one on your genitals. Stay with you your breath for a couple minutes as you absorb the energy of this experience and witness your thoughts, emotions and sensations.

Hygiene, Safety and Ethics

This is a topic that often comes up once people's other questions and fears have been addressed relative to the emotional content of genital massage practice.

It is odd to me that people would be more concerned about emotional responses than health issues. While obviously I do not discount the importance of emotions, I know emotions are fleeting and I can choose how to respond to my emotions. I trust myself to handle any emotion that comes up, whether that be fear, jealousy, disgust, etc. I also trust myself to be able to handle being in the presence of another's emotions. I know that I can choose to remain calm and grounded even if someone else is in extreme emotional distress. I may not always remain totally grounded, but I know I have the capacity to do so.

When I think about a sexual partner engaging in sexual activity with another person, I am mostly concerned about health issues and whether, in my judgment, my risk of contracting a Sexually Transmitted Disease or other disease has significantly increased do to my partner's activity. Am I more at risk of HIV/AIDS? Of Herpes? Of other serious diseases? For me, I cannot enjoy sexual activity if I think I am engaging in a high-risk or even medium risk activity. And I cannot enjoy myself if I think I may be exposing someone else to risk from me.

My ethics require me to fully share all information I have about myself and to keep my partner informed if I have connected sexually with anyone else since we were together last. For me to experience trust and openness, I want the same from my partner. I want to know explicitly if they have had sexual connections with another person or persons. I want to know the details of what physically transpired so I can determine whether I am at a significantly increased health risk or not.

You can get a good chart of STD risk from a chart compiled by the San Francisco Department of Health. From the chart it is clear that some activities are high risk, such as penis/anal penetration with no barrier such as a condom. Slightly less high risk is penis/vagina penetration with no condom. Using a condom is so effective at stemming the risk of HIV/AIDS that the City Clinic will not use the resources to test people if they have been using condoms.

For genital massage, we use our hands to provide manual stimulation of the genitals. This is a very low risk activity. Of course the hands should be clean, using hot soapy water to thoroughly clean them before starting a session and after concluding a session. That is probably sufficient to prevent the spread of any diseases as long as there are not cuts on the hands.

You can even go a step further and use gloves for every session. This is even safer and offers practically 100% protection from any type of transmission. If I had any type of cut or abrasion on my hand, or if I knew the person I was touching was at higher risk of an STD or had one, I would use gloves.

I've seen people insist on gloves for genital massage even while engaging in much higher-risk activity with a lover than a practice partner. This is probably due to emotional factors such as wanting a lower degree of intimacy with their practice partner than their lover. But in terms of STD risk, it is totally irrational.

My desire for myself and everyone else is to enjoy as much sensation and enjoyment and emotional connection with as little health risk as possible. And I want everyone to be empowered in asking for what they want. Some people are more willing to accept high-risk activities than others. And some people may want to have different practices with different people due to their emotions. Everyone can become aware of their choices and conscious of why they are making them. This is more important than everyone making the same choices.

In the bigger picture, consciousness is the best protection we can use.

CHAPTER 5:
Giving Sexual Healing & Empowerment Sessions

Disclaimer:
This chapter describes, in partial detail, the work I do. I do not suggest after reading the section that you begin doing this work, as there is much more study and experience that goes into conducting a professional sensual or sexual healing career. If you are interested in pursuing this career-path, I suggest doing at least one in-depth training program that includes hands-on work as well as on-going mentoring as you developing your practice. Working with several different teachers and practitioners will enhance your knowledge and give you the experience you need to powerfully enter this field.

If you are mainly interested in learning this for your own benefit and the benefit of your partner or lovers, go ahead and experiement with this material in your personal relationships.

Integrity and Staying Grounded

"To live outside the law you must be honest" – Bob Dylan

I come into contact with people who are doing various forms of sex work. There are quite a few people, mainly women, who do sensual massage, which may or may not integrate tantra or other approaches to sacred sexuality.

Typically, men are the ones drawn to pay for this type of service, although more and more women are looking for, and are willing to pay for, services from a man who can assist them to have an experience they want. Often, people are not sure of exactly what they want.

Working in this field requires that I know my own desires, boundaries, patterns. It is essential to have total clarity about my offerings. It is very important to remember to do only what I want to do. I am not leasing my body out to someone to use as they please, and I am consciously providing services that are in alignment with my goal to create a more joyful, compassionate and connected world.

I remember doing sessions with a friend of mine years ago. We were doing a "double," as it is known in the trade. We were massaging the client together and I remember clearly a moment where I had the temptation to "check out" and unilaterally surrender to the client's desire. It was one of those important points in life – a fork in the road – and I realize now how important it was that I chose not to surrender.

A big part of the turn-on for many people sexually, is the sense of power they receive. The ability to have someone fulfill your desire is as much of a thrill as the actual doing of it. I was doing another double with the same friend and she was stroking me. At one point the client expressed a desire for something and my partner said, "I don't think he wants to, but I'll ask him."

This was an example of bringing greater consciousness into sexuality. By modeling our communication and respect for each other, we showed the client how it is possible to be honest, communicative and respectful and still have a hot sexual interaction. For so many people who subconsciously separate their sexual desires and their desire for love, acceptance and connection, this is very important.

To help heal this separation in our lovers, our partners or our clients, we need to have the intention to be whole ourselves. The more we can speak our desires and boundaries without judgment the more we can integrate them into our lives. Then our turn on arises from increased consciousness and connection, not fantasies that leave our hearts and minds at the door.

But if you are doing hands-on work in the sensual field there will often be a temptation to give a client what they think they want. Similarly, many partners just give in to their partner's sexual desires without acknowledging it is not what they want. It takes lot of strength to say no and to mark our boundaries without making them wrong. I have a friend who when she hears that a client wants to have sex with her will say, "Oh, you want a full-service provider. I can give you a referral." This is done without judgment, efficiently and helpfully.

It is important to note that in this field we often work with clients we would not spend time with if we were not getting paid. So where is the line between working for money and working in alignment with our highest purpose? My approach is to always state and hold my intention to provide clients with my being, my love, my compassion and my consciousness. I do not make promises of what I will do. I always retain my freedom to choose.

If someone is only looking for a body to play a role in their dramatic fantasy, I encourage them to look for a match who shares their fantasy. I am not an actor. I offer myself as a real person who is only doing what I want to do and is in alignment with my sense of self and my highest intentions.

So many of us have been conditioned by the sex-negative culture to only get turned on by being "bad" or by "checking out." This is taking the easy way out, and practicing sex in this way will ultimately drain our energy. It is abdicating our responsibility to ourselves and the result is often fear of facing some repressed emotion or experience. People who were sexually abused as children learned to dissociate or "check out" of their bodies and find a safe place in their minds. I've seen many a sex worker with a history of sexual abuse use this ability to give clients what they want, essentially renting out their body while they check out for a while. This is a very dangerous because they leave themselves open to indiscriminate activity and surrender their ability to make conscious choices.

Conversely, many people who do this work are very clear about who they are and what they do. The work is very useful in helping people draw their boundaries, discover their desires, and improve their ability to communicate with reference to self without judgment or charge.

The danger is that we may think we have done our work and are acting consciously but are still in unconscious reaction to unexamined material from our past. To ensure against that, it is crucial to have a community around us to whom we are comfortable opening up to and receive reflections on ourselves. It is a valuable gift to have people in our lives with whom we can intimately share ourselves, and to trust that their reflections of us are motivated by love and compassion.

How do we discern who has this intention and ability to connect compassionately? The more we trust and reveal ourselves, the more we come into the present moment without being influenced by our subconscious desires and patterns. The more we trust ourselves, the more we can trust others.
 The more we are in the present moment the greater our ability to perceive others and discern their intentions.
I remember a number of years back after I separated from my wife, how amazed I was at my newly found psychic abilities. I was not helping solve crimes or bending spoons with my mind, but I was far more in tune with others and able to intuit what was going on in their lives.

Years ago, I had a session in Los Angeles with a woman I had never met or worked with before. A Middle Eastern woman in her 30's, she wanted someone to help her orgasm. She was beautiful young, exotic—and wealthy. We talked on the phone for a few minutes and set up and appointment for later the same day. As she drove in from Beverly Hills I set up the session room, preparing not only the space but also myself.

The act of cleaning, clearing and organizing the place of work can be very useful in helping to clear us emotionally. After getting set up, I sat and breathed, allowing myself to express anything to myself I needed to release to come into the present moment. I set my intentions and any special boundaries I had for this particular session. Being clear and grounded this way, I was able to sit and breathe and meditate until the client arrived.

When she arrived, I opened the door and was struck by her beauty and her nervousness. When she was comfortably seated I asked her to tell me why she was here and what she hoped to gain from the session. I listened to her describe her sexuality and her inability to orgasm. She was married with children but had never had an orgasm.

After she described herself, her life and her reasons for seeing me I gave her an outline of what I had in mind for the session. Each session is unique and it is important to be open to the flow of the moment, sensing where the energy is, and what may be useful rather than following a set formula.

I remember how rigid she was. As I touched her, she seemed to have no response. When I was stroking her clitoris, she said she could not discern any sensation at all. This is actually common. Many women have shut down their sexuality and cannot experience much if any sensation from their genitals. Living in the sexual training center focused on stroking, I knew many women who took a month or more of daily sessions before they could begin to truly experience sensation in their clitoris.

Many people have never had the experience of lying down and doing nothing but breathing and paying attention to their genitals. So often the emotions associated with sex, excitement, fear, attraction and disgust, overwhelm our ability to sense what our body is experiencing on the level of sensation. So a big key to opening and expanding sexually, and increasing our conscious awareness, is the experience of focusing on pure sensation.

Of course emotions do come up, often very strongly, in these sessions. When set against a background of deep, slow breathing and attention to sensation, we can experience emotions that have been locked up for a long time. To be held in this way and to receive completely from another person who has no agenda but to be of service, can be very healing. Whether the session involves meditation and eye-gazing, holding or cuddling, clit stroking or intercourse, the important thing is for the client to receive fully and use the opportunity to go where they want and need to go, while respecting the boundaries of the service provider.

So many women have not had the experience of a man holding space for them without pushing his own agenda. This experience can be very healing, bringing up tears of sadness for all the times their needs were not met.

Taking time and going very slowly expands the sense of time and the range of sensation possible. Increase attention, not pressure or speed. When we go very slowly, each stroke up the clit can take ½ a minute or more, we increase the sense of size of the area that is being stroked. It is as if we are literally enlarging that part of our body through careful and deliberate stroking

Initially, the middle-eastern woman could perceive very little sensation in her clitoris. She was accustomed to fast, rough sex from her husband, likely learned from pornography and reinforced by a male-dominated, sex-negative culture. She asked me to fuck her. After I checked in with myself, I told her I would enter her but would not reinforce her pattern of rough, fast, disassociated sex. I encouraged her to breathe, to relax and notice what sensations, emotions and thought were emerging from her.

This was challenging for her. Her pattern of fast, hard fucking focused on bringing her man to orgasm was so strong she did not know how to please herself. She was uncomfortable in moments when I was not moving. She knew how to be the passive recipient of male energy, but had never experienced active feminine energy that draws in the male energy.

Looking back on it, while I didn't do anything "wrong", I realize now that she needed more than just a sensitive, communicative lover or a sweet sexual experience. She needed to connect with her own body and emotions and learn how to move and touch her own body to release her emotions before we engaged in touch with me or anyone else.

If I were to see her today, we would likely have several sessions of talking and moving emotions before engaging in any touch. While the session gave her an experience to help open her sexually, the primary emphasis should be on the emotional body so the physical experience can be integrated.

It is very important to use session work to experience ecstasy, freedom and bliss, but also to use the opportunity to see our patterns, gain greater awareness of our motives and desires, and experiment with different ways of relating.

Another session around this same time was very different. She was an older woman, a single professional who was very sex-positive. She asked me for a session after attending one of my workshops, and wanted to role-play with me. She wanted me to restrain her, roll around on top of her, and basically simulate a rape fantasy without actually raping her. All the while she remained conscious of her process and I repeatedly checked in with her. This is intense, challenging work that requires absolute integrity and a high degree of awareness and sensitivity. When we doing this type of session, we are creating a scene that is very familiar and yet doing it in a different way so as to shift the patterns of behavior and create more freedom of response for the client.

In all of these sessions no matter how different they are, it is crucial for both the practitioner and the client to be in touch at all times with their intentions, desires and goals, and to communicate without hesitation or reservation. Empowered relating is the key to healing no matter what issue is being worked on or what methods are employed.

Empowerment and Deep Listening

I first started doing conscious sexual work, as opposed to just "making out" for fun and connecting with those I love, when I lived at a sexuality training center in San Francisco. The community's mission focused on expanding the female orgasm. The primary practice for expanding female orgasm in this specific model is clitoral massage that consists of having a partner stroke the upper left quadrant of the female receiver's clitoris for 15 minutes. As I previously described, this can be a very effective practice for giving pleasure and for gaining familiarity and ease with a woman's body, her responses, as well as with one's self as the giver.

What I found was that this was not the cure-all for every issue, both sexual and non-sexual that women and men endure. To posit that, as the center seemed to do, was to raise the practice to an ideology. When a woman was in distress, mad, sad, confused, etc., the founder's advice would be "Go stroke pussy."

This could be received as encouragement or permission that enabled one to focus on pleasure and that can be very helpful. But it also can be a match to addictive behavioral patterns. Were we just substituting clitoral stimulation for other addictions? Were people actually moving through their distress, recognizing their patterns, and having happier, more connected, more compassion in their lives? The results were mixed.

I was amazed to see the level of confidence and embodiment that emerged in some women after a relatively short period of time of following this practice. Others, even after several years, did not seem to shift their behavioral patterns that much. This center included other practices such as varied communication games, but the overwhelming focus was on stroking the clitoris.

The lack of emotional intimacy at this sexuality training center was a significant impediment to greater relaxation, connection and healing. For a place devoted to female orgasm, the emphasis was strongly on stimulation, power and intellect, and there was no commitment or intention for non-violent language or even physical safety. The leader would often say, "There is no safety." Which is certainly true in the absolute sense: we are all going to die, and sometimes things that hurt us are out of our control. But we can set an *intention* for safety, non-violence and to assist others in peril.

I left the sexuality training center after being assaulted by one of the long-time members of the community. He was a huge ex-marine who nearly pushed me through a set of glass doors. More disturbing to me than his actions, which were certainly disturbing, was the reactions of others in the community. One man witnessed this from the other side of the locked doors and refused to act when I directly asked him to intervene. And when I spoke to the founder about it, asking if the community had an intention for non-violence, she said no. I asked her main assistant and he said that even though he did not witness the incident he trusted the ex-marine implicitly. After hearing that, I packed my bags and left. I had "graduated."

When I think about that incident in the context of sexuality, I realize that, for me, a key ingredient in healing and empowerment work is a conscious intention for everyone's physical safety and wellbeing. People do get hurt and injured but my understanding of compassion is that we try to minimize suffering. That is why it is important to check in repeatedly during sessions to make sure the client is present in their body, mind and emotions.

What I wanted was an approach to sexual healing that would be responsive to the individual needs and desires of the receiver. Rather than putting energy into following a specific protocol every time I did a session as we did at the center in San Francisco, I developed the conscious sensuality approach, which is a form of deep listening that gives the receiver the experience of being heard. This lack of listening, I believe, was one of the deepest wounds that the clitoral massage at the training center, or any ideological, cookie-cutter approach could not heal. To heal this wound, the receiver must be supported and encouraged to ask for exactly what they want, and the giver must practice deep and active listening; listening both to the receiver and to himself or herself to make sure that their giving is in alignment with their desires and boundaries.

When one is receiving sexual touch or any type of massage or healing work, the receiver has the choice of how much to voice their desires and make requests regarding what they are receiving. For many, a major piece of empowerment is to practice speaking clearly and asking precisely for what they want. It is also important to recognize that some people have a pattern of over-verbalizing and trying to control every aspect of the experience while they are receiving. This is not so much empowerment as a patterned response to fear of losing control. If you sense this pattern in someone, it is more useful to probe deeper to release the roots of this fear. It is crucial that you have entered into an agreement field with your client or lover so you can voice your perceptions in a manner that builds love, trust and understanding.

Entering the Agreement Field

If one trusts themselves to speak when something is painful, uncomfortable or seems really out of place, they can turn their mind and word machine off and simply experience what is happening in the body while receiving. In order to encourage this level of connection and opening to this non-verbal experience, trust needs to paramount.

To help do this, I like to create an agreement field that is a set of agreements we make at the beginning of a session or a workshop. The agreements I suggest can be altered or added to according to the needs and desires of the people involved. This is crucial because if the agreement field is always the same it is not a partnership that integrates what is needed but a static or rigid agreement that does not honor each person's uniqueness.

The agreements I suggest for the agreement field are:
1. To be 100% responsible for your choices at all times.
2. To maintain confidentiality about other's identities and experiences.
3. To be coachable and willing to receive feedback.

4. To be present, and not under the influence of drugs or alcohol immediately before, during or after the session or course.

To clarify, being coachable does not mean blindly do what is asked, but listening and considering the advice or encouragement without reacting immediately and unconsciously. This is crucial because when we come up to an old pattern a block will likely emerge. We need to breathe, pause and feel into whether we are in fear and resistance or not.

When to Focus on the G-spot

In tantra circles I have also experienced an overemphasis on "sacred spot" work, which contrary to the aforementioned training center's model, focuses on internal stimulation of the G-spot, including the male G-spot wherein internal pressure is used while stroking the prostate gland. While this work can be deeply healing and empowering, it can also be a similar one-size fits all approach to sexual healing. It will fail if healing is done solely on the physical plane without integrating the emotional level.

Being held and supported as we release old trauma, pain, muscle armor and fear is more important that skillful stimulation to bring about a cathartic emotional release through the buildup of tension. Be wary of sexual healers that act with arrogance or have supreme confidence that they know what you need.

People need to feel safe, heard and respected. Stroking skills and charisma are not a substitute for a healer who is more of a guide and an ally rather than a mechanic or salesman. Activating the G-spot of a woman who has not taken responsibility for herself, who has not reached a level of empowerment and awareness, invites projection, blame, and calcification of old, dysfunctional patterns rooted in fear. This is why it is important as a healer to have a sense of where someone is on his or her journey.

Better to go slow and do little to nothing on the physical plane. By asking questions and proving we are responsive to the needs and desires of the client, we build trust that we are doing this work to serve them and not ourselves, our desire, our egos, or merely for the cash flow. Because people have such a strong need for emotional release and a desire for ecstasy, sacred spot work can be very powerful, pleasurable and cathartic. But when and how is it actually healing, empowering and transformative?

I am not in judgment of anyone when I write this, but in a place of deep questioning: What are the most effective means and approaches to sexual healing and empowerment? If you only have "healing" without empowerment, I doubt the healing is going to result in transformative change. And if the focus is solely on emotional release, talk therapy/psychoanalysis and no touch, most people will not re-pattern their sexuality. Working on the physical plane with a guide who does not have attachment or focus on their own desires and who sets an intention for your healing can be much more helpful than just exploring sexually with someone without training and awareness. Just as both the feminine and masculine energies are needed for the universe to function, both are required in developing a healthy and empowered sexuality.

Consent and Informed Consent

An important concept in this work is the distinction of consent vs. informed consent. The distinction is rooted in the understanding that one can give consent without knowing to what one is consenting. This was helpful to me when I tried to understand a session I did with a young woman who asked me to help her resolve her inability to orgasm. She was young, about 20 years old, and very beautiful. I was happy and excited when she agreed to do a session. When we first met, she gave me a big hug and cuddled up next to me on the couch. She had come with a male daka, an apprenticing male tantric healer. she confided that he had encouraged her to attend the conference we were at. She had a boyfriend at home who she loved very much but with whom she could not orgasm.

I was aware of my level of attraction to her and I wanted to be transparent and in total integrity. It is a tricky situation when one is attracted to a client. Some believe that if attracted to a potential client, one should not work with them as this could get in the way of holding space for them, or result in a conscious or subconscious attempt to get them to fall in love with you. On the other hand, the energy of your attraction can serve as energy for transformation if used with awareness and skill.

I think a crucial distinction can be made between attraction, even strong sexual attraction, and a desire to have a romantic or partnership relationship. If I see someone as a potential lover, I need to make a choice: Do I want this person as a lover and possibly a partner, or as a client? It is possible for a client to later become a lover, but not too likely the other way around. And if a healer starts a sexual relationship with someone who is attracted to them partially on the basis of their healing skills, they could be depriving the client of the opportunity to fully dive into their growth and healing by *not* pursuing a practitioner-client relationship.

If someone is in need of sexual healing it is natural that they could be attracted to the practitioner. And of course people would rather have a romantic relationship than pay for sessions. But session work can be invaluable to personal growth. It is important to move beyond the ego's ideas about paying for a session. Many people see the idea of paying for a session as akin to paying for sex that would cast the receiver in an inferior position.

On the other hand, you can see paying for a session as an act of empowerment; I want to work on some issues and by paying for a session or sessions I'm giving myself a gift. The ego could just as easily see the giver in an inferior position in that they are providing their service for money. Because of historical inequities and the patriarchal oppression, women are seen as the victims more often that men, regardless of whether they are paying or getting paid for session.

Developing a Personal Ethical Framework

When I am attracted to a client I have to make an evaluation also for myself: Do I want to do sessions with this person, or do I want to explore a mutual relationship with them? And of course, my needs for love, sex, companionship and money could impact the decision. My intention, however, is that money, desire for sex, love and relationship not influence my decision-making.

I make a distinction between doing work that I would not do for free and doing things just for money. The distinction is crucial because I have to believe that I am doing a service and benefitting others. If I am just doing something for money, it is far too easy to start violating my own boundaries and this can be dangerous spiritually, psychologically, emotionally and even physically because we are talking about sex, which carries risk of sexually transmitted diseases.

To support my health and safety I consider what I am doing to be health work more than sex work. I see what I am doing as helping others become healthier in regard to their bodies, sexuality, emotions and relationships. Sexuality and pleasure are valued, but within the service of the larger goals of health, healing and empowerment.

So when I had this beautiful young woman coming to see me because she wanted to have help finding her orgasm, it was a challenge for me to stay present and be a valuable source of support for her. I also felt challenged to stay in integrity, speak my truth, acknowledge my desire, and really give to her instead of taking from her.

This last one was the biggest challenge because the pattern is so strong in our culture. Beautiful young women are a much sought after commodity in our sexual marketplace. The commodification of sex and the objectification of woman as well as the desensitization of men from their sensual nature results in a culture where women are expected to be beautiful and sexy, but not easy or slutty. And men are expected to need beautiful young women to fulfill them sexually rather than sourcing their own pleasure from within.

Disconnection and Dissociation

Because beautiful young women often have men approaching them, they usually develop shields to protect themselves. These shields, unless constructed consciously, can become fixed internal blocks and may even show up physically as muscle tension, contraction and pain or even more serious medical conditions. This can become a serious impediment to a woman's natural joy and ease in her body. This can also result in the inability to orgasm and a host of other issues such as vaginismus, painful intercourse, stuck emotions, etc.

If a woman has suffered sexual abuse or trauma, she may be orgasmic and very sexually active but dissociate or disconnect during sex and experience trouble in developing intimacy and trust with her sexual partner/s. This can result in the familiar "fucking or fighting" relationship where there is little besides these two options. It may look passionate and sexy, but it is not deeply nourishing and healing. There needs to be more options for women than the Madonna or the whore.

A big part of the role of a guide in a sexual healing and empowerment session is to help the receiver remain connected to themselves and to the present moment and their surroundings. When we *dissociate* we lose touch with where we are or what we are doing. When we *disconnect*, we lose connection with ourselves or those around us. For many people, sex mainly happens through dissociating or disconnecting, when they lose the inhibitions and armor that they developed to protect themselves. When we become more conscious and develop trust in ourselves, we can *choose* when to have certain boundaries rather than walking around with a clunky suit of armor at all times.

What Would a Sex-Positive Culture Look Like?

In a sex-obsessed and repressed culture few people take the time for deeply nourishing, bonding connected sex. The emphasis is usually either on super-hot mind-blowing sex with unbelievably intense orgasms or non-erotic sweet cuddly friendships with little sex.

Many people have a hard time connecting sexually without the influence of drugs or alcohol. It is socially acceptable to go to a bar or a fraternity party or a high-class cocktail party, dress up in a sexy outfit and be very flirtatious. Yet if someone says they are going to go to a group that is consciously exploring sexuality without any drugs or alcohol many would see them as sex obsessed, weird or even feared as members of some "cult."

"Hey Mom, I'm going out now to my sexual exploration group. I'll be back by 10pm." How would that sound to you as a parent? Your daughter, age 16, is going out for the evening. She is not going to drink or smoke pot. She is going to gather with some friends who will talk about their emotions, their desires, do some cuddling and massage and perhaps practice some sexual exploration and play. They will do this with condoms and gloves, discuss their STD status and any concerns they have. They will talk about their emotions, make requests and respect boundaries. This is the world in which I want to live; where everyone, including kids under 18, is supported in their sexual exploration, enjoyment and empowerment.

Do this sound like a bizarre universe? It does not have to sound as such. Do you have a daughter? Are you really hoping that her first sexual contact will be on her wedding night? Is that for her good or to deal with your fear, shame and guilt around sexuality?

Approaching a Sexual Healing and Empowerment Session

For those already sexually active in a sex-negative culture and those who experience fear, shame and guilt related to sex, they may benefit from a series of sexual healing and empowerment sessions. Rather than try to convince people to do this work, it is enough to hold space and articulate our intentions, vision and willingness to explore this realm with those who feel called to do this work. This is not a cure-all, nor is it the most effective approach to all issues or all people. But we have developed an approach that has helped many people with greater sexual healing and empowerment.

If someone is interested in doing a session or learning more, communicate with them and find out what they want to work on. Send them an intake form that is designed to start their process of sexual healing and empowerment. Some people benefit just from reading the intake form and never doing a session. Others may not feel ready to do such intimate work. It is important to make no attempt to convince anyone to do anything or promise any results. It is important to be humble and acknowledge the other person's self-knowledge and choices.

By having an intake form, I let the client know that I take my work seriously and am a professional. While pleasure is very important and can be very healing, the intake form communicates that my service is distinct from simply a sensual massage session.

Completing an intake process establishes the client as an active participant in their healing and empowerment. Reading the form, the after-session guide as well as the FAQ sheet will stimulate them mentally and emotionally before we ever make physical contact. I like to send the intake form several days before a session. By the time a client has their appointment they have been in session with themselves for several days.

Writing down answers to questions on the form may bring emotional releases and more consciousness to what they are really seeking. If their answers are unclear I will ask about them and if something seems really important we will discuss it more extensively.

Talk Therapy Only Goes So Far

As much as building connection, trust and a shared language is a crucial foundation for later work, talk only gets a client so far. That is why they are coming to see me and not a psychotherapist or counselor. They want to explore more embodied practices for reclaiming their health, pleasure and joy in life.

Again, people tend to be drawn toward approaches that reinforce their stories and patterns. So for many people doing talk therapy may only serve to make the neurotic and self-obsessed even more intense.

Have you ever talked with someone who has gone to therapy for a long time? They can recite chapter and verse about their own psychology and yet seem unaware of how to *change* their patterns. They know what is wrong but they do not know how to fix themselves. It can be a form of hypochondria; people are comfortable with the pain they know. They identify with their disease, and it becomes part of who they are.

Instead of adopting practices that serve their health and growth they focus on the mental activity of learning how they are screwed up. There is much more to say about disease, health, ailments and abnormalities. Health is health. Why talk about it? If you are healthy, go for a bike ride, fly a kite, do yoga, make love and have fun. If you have a problem or a disease, do something about it, do not just think about it.

How Can You Find a Sexual Healer?

OK, you say, I want to work on my sexual issues, how do I do that? Because of the stigma and legalities attached to work involving direct, embodied sexuality, people often do not know where to turn. Should I see a counselor, a priest, a therapist or…a sex worker? Going to see a priest about a sexual problem is like going to see a lawyer about your skin condition.

Out of all the people doing paid sex work, many are focused on providing pleasure or addiction-maintenance. If they are doing addiction-maintenance work, they are likely unaware or un-empowered in regard to their own addiction issues which is why they are aligned with sex-addicted clients. To find someone who is a match to your desire for healing and empowerment requires more than just throwing the dice and contacting one of thousands who advertise their services.

Look for someone that has done training in counseling, communication, meditation, and other personal development work. Find someone who has done their own healing and will talk about it. Use your own intuition, beware of your tendency to give away your power and hope someone will heal you. You are in charge of your own healing journey.

The Intake Form
I first give or send my clients an intake form with the following questions:

"What is the name you like to be called?"
"What is your phone number and email address?"
"What is your occupation?"

"Do you have any previous or current illnesses or medical conditions including STD's?"
"Do you take any medications or drugs, legal or illegal on a regular basis including alcohol, marijuana, tobacco, caffeine, sleep aids, anti-depressants, etc.?"
"Describe your current emotional state:"
"Describe any sexual trauma or abuse you have experienced, including verbal:"
"Do you have any ongoing sexual relationships?"
"What issues are you experiencing in these relationship(s)?"
"What is your primary intention for our sessions?"

And most importantly:

"Sometimes painful emotions or sensations arise and it is up to you to decide if you want to pause or stop or if you want to work through them and release them.
Will you tell me immediately and clearly if you are experiencing pain, discomfort or want a pause or a stop to the session?"

For me to proceed and feel safe I need to hear an unequivocal agreement to this last question, and so I will ask again in person at the start of a session. If the answer is not 100% yes, we will talk until I am satisfied that they have reached this base level of awareness and empowerment. Of course, a significant responsibility of the practitioner is attunement to when the clients is not aware of their emotions or body and needs a pause but doesn't ask for one. Doing sexual healing work is fraught with many perils: legal, financial, relationships, health and more.

Doing a thorough intake process is important to protecting oneself and serving the client.

Clearing the Emotional Field Before Touch

Besides the written questions on the intake form which we may discuss in more detail at the beginning of work with a client, I usually also ask a series of questions designed to build trust, connection and greater awareness and self-responsibility. I may ask:

1) Do you need to say or release anything to be more present for this session?

This is where it is important to listen and probe if necessary if I sense anything that is unsaid. Especially if I sense there is any material related to me such as fear, attraction, etc.

2) Will you tell me if anything is painful, uncomfortable or you want a pause or end to the session?

The answer must be a vocalized, unequivocal "Yes" to proceed.

3) Do you have an intention for this session that you want to speak or say silently to yourself?

4) Do you have any boundaries for this session that you want to state at this time?

5) If yes, do you want me to support your boundaries even if you change your mind?

This last one is very important as receivers may gradually open up and relax and enjoy the session so that may change their boundaries during the session. It is important to hold clients to their own boundaries to protect myself from post-session contractions of fear, shame and guilt. Better to go slow.

Moving Beyond Reflexive "No's" and Inauthentic "Yes's"

Remember, if you are working with women, they have likely been indoctrinated to believe they should not desire touch, pleasure and sex. They may state a boundary that is not reflective of a true desire but in an attempt to maintain the appearance of a "good girl." This is habitual for some women and why they need support and encouragement in reclaiming their bodies, their choices and their self-respect.

Communicate that it is natural for them to want touch, sex, pleasure and orgasms. Do not attempt to give them something you think they want, even if they change their mind unless they have reserved the right to change their minds. You can always do another session at another time. If they are disappointed or frustrated by you holding their boundary it may help them to reevaluate their patterns and encourage them to take responsibility for their words and to trust that a man will honor their boundaries even when they are not honoring themselves.

Dropping Into Deeper Levels of Touch

One of the ways to communicate and encourage awareness and respect is by paying attention to the various levels of intimate touching that are possible. Just as the goal in massage is not to go as deeply as possible, but to find the depth of pressure that is just right, the goal in sexual healing and empowerment is to find the appropriate level of physical intimacy.

This cannot be taught but must be learned through practice. It is important to recognize that we are all born with a natural desire for touch. From our desire for breast milk and cuddling to vigorous sexual intercourse, we want touch. And at times we need space to heal, to integrate and to rest to be in solitude and celibacy. Most of the time, we could enjoy and benefit from more touch, and more intimate touch—a long, slow, melting hug as opposed to a quick, rigid, A-frame hug.

The key to dropping in to deeper levels of physically and sexually intimate touch is to be aware when new levels are being entered and to be sensitive to how these different levels may be experienced by the receiver. We live a culture that has been influenced by the binary nature of either/or, yes/no and on/off choices. Cultivating sensitivity and developing a more fluid, more lyrical approach to sensuality and sexuality invites us to go beyond the binary model.

It is another way we can practice moving more and more into a state of conscious response rather that unconscious reaction. Sensuality is an opportunity to develop our free will and exquisite sensitivities to others and ourselves.

There are numerous levels of intimate physical touch, and many more levels and refinements on those levels. You can think of the levels as plateaus or mesas from which to savor the view. Conscious attention and enjoyment of different levels is a key part of unlearning the culturally indoctrinated race to vigorous intercourse. With the easy accessibility and omnipresence of sexually explicit videos on the web, millions of people internalize the message that sex is fast hard fucking and little else. There are certainly more alternatives to this than just abstinence and celibacy.

When we were kids and just starting to explore sexually, we used sports analogies such as first base for kissing, second base for breast touch, third base for genital touch or oral sex and home run for fucking. This also reinforces the mindset that the end goal is fucking, which is not always what is truly desired or even the most enjoyable experience at all times. What is the mutual intersection of desire? That is where we find the most energy and connection.

Until we have sexually explicit videos that portray a different approach and type of sexuality, this is what we will deal with in our culture. Why not allow children to watch loving, sensitive beautiful lovemaking? If they are not interested they will not watch it. If they are interested, why not show that instead of the millions of mindless sport-fucking videos out there?

Why not educate teenagers on the various levels of intimate touch rather than leave them to explore in the dark. Imagine a course that teaches and perhaps even engages students in various forms of touch. The curriculum might include:

1) Fully clothed both giver and receiver with no direct physical contact.
2) Fully clothed both giver and receiver with some physical contact but no touch in the genital region.
3) Receiver partially or totally nude with giver clothed or unclothed and gives non-genital touch.
4) Receiver invites a hand to be place near the genital area but without physical contact as a means to perceive and integrate energetically.
5) Receiver invites direct genital contact without movement as a means to physically ground energy. This can be done with or without clothing and with or without gloves.
6) Receiver invites direct genital contact and movement. This can be limited to external genital contact or be internal as well.

I find that a lot of direct G-spot pressure and stimulation without whole body touch may repeat patterns of dissociation and disconnection. The focus of this work is healing and empowerment. I work with givers, both men and women, to release any attachment they have toward orgasm, ejaculation or peak states in the receiver. After trust and connection is built over several sessions, more people can experiment with more vigorous G-spot stimulation, but I do not advise it in a first session. That is more advanced work.

A similar multi-level approach to chest and breast touch is also helpful. For breast touch, consider these options:

1) Receiver is fully clothed and the giver places a hand near but not touching their heart.
2) Receiver is fully clothed and brings the giver's hand to rest on their heart.
3) Receiver does the same with no clothing above the waist.
4) Giver massages the unclothed side of the body from the armpit to the waist, passing over the side of the breast and integrating it with the rest of the body. This is a very important stroke that helps to detoxify the breast and when done regularly, may help prevent breast cancer.
5) Giver massages the breast directly but does not touch the nipples
6) Giver massages the breasts directly including the nipples but does not focus attention on the nipples. This is similar to the side breast-stroke that integrates the nipple into the rest of the breast energetically.
7) Giver massages the breasts and focuses attention on the nipples, stimulating them with different motions such as squeezing, rolling, pinching and twisting as invited by the receiver.

For a man receiving prostate massage:

1) Bring your hand close to but not touching the genital region on a clothed receiver.
2) Bring your hand to rest over the genital region which is clothed.
3) Invite the man to disrobe entirely and place your hand over the genitals.
4) Massage the testicles, perineum and lingam in a slow meditative manner
5) Increase the pressure and speed on the lingam without bringing him to ejaculation.
6) Make contact with the anus and slowly massage it
7) Insert your finger and let it rest on the prostate.
8) Make slow rhythmic strokes on the prostate

Ethics Regarding Intimate Touch

In much of the obsessed and repressed western world, there is fear, shame and guilt that accompanies intimate physical touch and prohibitions and penalties associated with certain types of touch. In our sexualized culture, many people see *all* touch as sexual. This has resulted in a severe lack of non-sexual physical intimacy and nurturing touch.

Gaining more experience and perspective on intimate, genital and sexual touch can help people distinguish between different types of touch. By focusing on and inviting in exploration of more intimate, genital and sexual touch, we help people to become more comfortable asking for, getting and giving the type of touch they want.

Would a sexually satisfied person rape or molest? There are deep psychological issues involved, particularly power and ego dynamics, but the more we can shine light with open talk about and practice conscious sexuality and the more non-sexual loving and nurturing touch we have, the less shadow will emerge due to hunger and thirst from its dark cave.

I know a woman who was dealing with a child custody issue with her ex-husband and the judge ordered the woman not to be naked in front of her own children. And this was in California, supposedly the center of permissiveness and sex-positive culture! I cannot imagine what harm it would do for children to see their own mother naked. I can understand that a father or others would not want children to see their parent having sex, I may not agree, but I can understand it. But I cannot understand linking nudity to sexuality.

I live next to a nude beach and I see far more provocative sexual behavior on the beaches were women are wearing less than a roll of dental floss. Barely covering up the breasts and genitals only draws attention to them as opposed to seeing them as natural and beautiful parts of an integrated whole.

Just as the dental-floss bikinis titillate more than they cover up, our obsession with sex in the legal system obscures the need for the development of personal ethics and responsibility and sensitivity. If it is legal, go for it with no other thought. If it is illegal, do not do it or we will punish you. This is another either/or system with little thought and much projection behind it.

Sex Magic and Shamanism

Many people working in the field of sacred sexuality utilize terms such as magic, shamanism and spirituality. There is much to be gained from non-linear, non-rational approaches and practices especially in regard to such a mysterious energy as sexuality. Delving into shamanic practices can help heal and open up energies and insights that talk therapy or bodywork alone do not reach.

One of the main dangers of magical and shamanic approaches though is the tendency for people to give up responsibility for their decisions and their awareness. Said another way, there is a fine line between entering a sexual shamanic trance and common patterns of dissociation and disconnection.

Shamanic work is advanced work. I only suggest trance work when you are well grounded and connected to yourself and present time reality. All too often, those most attracted to magic are those who are avoiding some unpleasant reality. Escapism in the form of sexuality is even more dangerous when we are deluding ourselves into thinking we are being healed by some powerful master.

I once saw a ritual demonstration of a shamanic sexual healing. There was no intake, no boundary setting and no checking in to see how the client was doing and what they were experiencing during the process. The whole thing reminded me of magician pulling a rabbit out of a yoni instead of a hat. It was a performance, not a healing. And this type of "sexual healing" work is more common than not unfortunately.

Towards an Erotic Ethics Forum

Here I note that in our efforts towards effective sexual healing and empowerment, we have no board or legal entity that licenses the practice. Unlike doctors, lawyers, massage therapists, psychologists, and many other professionals, those who do sexual healing work do so under a cloud of suspicion and the threat of fines, imprisonment or worse. Just doing sexual healing work that involves genital touch is considered illegal if money is exchanged in much of the world. Thankfully, many places now recognize that legal sex work is better for practitioners, clients and the community. Countries in Europe, Australia, New Zealand have revised laws. In California, the sexological bodywork and surrogacy programs have legitimized those doing healing sexual work.

And rather than attempt to distinguish sexual healers from prostitutes, let us leave the whole either/or baggage behind. Who is to say a person cannot have an amazingly beautiful experience with an escort? Some may be freaked out by a supposedly enlightened, sensitive tantrika with lots of credentials and testimonials.

Rather than codifying a set of must do's and don'ts with threats backed by government, I would like to see the development of an Erotic Ethics Forum for those involved in sex work of all stripes. Explicitly not having a punitive authority will encourage more open, honest dialogue and feedback. If you are interested in seeing what other's experiences with a healer were like, you could check out what others have to say about the practitioner with an online record of client's reviews. Then you could make an informed choice about who to see. And if you are a practitioner you could learn and grow and be less fearful about someone who has a challenging experience or projects their issues on you.

In our political systems, often the way to gain power, legitimacy and credibility is to distinguish your group from another group that is less organized and has less power. This happened as civil-rights leaders distinguished themselves from communists and socialists. Feminists distanced themselves from lesbians. Homosexuals distinguish themselves from Polyamorists. Polyamorists distance themselves from swingers. Let us not perpetuate this as sexual healers seek credibility by disavowing sex workers who have less privilege.

The Basic Sequence of a Conscious Sensuality Sexual Healing and Empowerment Session

Every session is different, but here is a general sequence:

- A potential client expresses interest in my work or a session.
- I discuss it with them to learn more about why they want to do a session.
- I give them an intake form and ask them to read some of my material.
- We set up an appointment for a time that allows them to prepare and to have enough spaciousness around the session for ease and integration.
- We start the session by connecting with ourselves, closing our eyes, breathing deeply and slowly and noticing our sensations, emotions and thoughts
- I go over the intake form and clarify any questions they have as well as inviting them to ask questions of me.
- Once we have addressed any issues or concerns either of us have we may move into physical contact or my discuss their issues, relationships, and sexuality with a focus on listening empathetically and allowing for emotional release.

We may begin physical touch with either hand-holding or a form of cuddling such as spooning. Dance and partner yoga are nice options too if there is nervousness. Both help calm nerves and build trust and connection as we move and express ourselves. Refrain from too much talking, as the point of this work is to become more embodied and not just release on a verbal or mental level.

It is also helpful to cuddle up, spoon and synchronize breathing. This happens less when we try to synchronize the breath, and more by relaxing and experiencing whatever sensations and emotions surface.

If this feels too intimate, facing each other and eye gazing is a great way to start building connection, trust and intimacy.

It is best to give a full-body massage before moving onto any genital contact. This is very helpful for relaxation and awakens their body to my touch. Again, I like to check in every so often to see if everything is ok. I will ask, "how's the pressure?" and, "is everything ok?" I also tell them explicitly that I will not touch their genitals unless they invite me to and that includes the breasts for women. This is very important because I want the client to feel as safe and relaxed as possible. And by clearly stating that genital contact is not going to happen without a clear request, I can touch close to the genitals and open the pelvic area without fear or contraction.

When I do sense they are ready for genital touch, I verbally ask if they would like to receive genital touch.   If I get a clear "yes" I will put my hand on their genitals slowly and hold it there for several breaths and make eye contact. Once we are grounded and connected, I can initiate movement if that is desired. I am very focused to make sure the client does not dissociate or disconnect during this part of the session. I ask, "How's the pressure?" How's the stroke?" and, "Do you want to continue?" This allows for a change of mind and encourages the receivers to check in with themselves.

If I sense there is some emotional material being uncovered, I'll continue with the same location, pressure, speed and motion...or if a really strong emotion is coming out I may go back to a still, grounding pressure without movement and make eye contact.

At the end of the session I give grounding, still pressure for several minutes to encourage energy absorption and emotional integration. This is a good time to rest and reflect. When it seems appropriate, I may ask if they want to describe anything that occurred for them during the session. It is beneficial to remain physically connected while speaking. This helps the client remain connected to their body and mind while speaking.

I go over the after-session guide and encourage them to follow up with an email or phone call in the next day or two. By encouraging reflection, journaling, emotional release work and other post-session activities, we expand the notion of the session to include all these elements beyond just the physical interaction that occurred. This is crucial for integration.

Repatterning Sexuality From a Sympathetic Response to a Parasympathetic Response

A major part of the nervous system is called the autonomic nervous system. This system is necessary for health and the well being of the human body as it maintains a state of balance. The autonomic nervous system is divided into two separate systems - the parasympathetic nervous system and the sympathetic nervous system. The sympathetic nervous system functions automatically and orchestrates the well-known responses of "fight or flight." The parasympathetic nervous system also functions automatically and cues the responses of relaxation.

The parasympathetic and sympathetic nervous systems usually function in opposition to one another, creating a balance within the systems of the human body. For example, when the heart receives neural stimulation from the parasympathetic nervous system, the heart slows down; on the contrary, when the heart receives neural stimulation from the neurons of the sympathetic nervous system, the heart speeds up.

The parasympathetic nervous system is deeply involved with the erectile tissue of the male and female - the penis and the clitoris, respectively. Then, dependent upon the proper function of the parasympathetic nervous system causing the erection, the sympathetic nervous system is responsible for the ejaculation or orgasm. This means that arousal is neurologically associated with relaxation.

This is crucial information because to create more relaxation and sex that is more than just a release of tension through ejaculation or orgasm, we need to support the parasympathetic response. This is why long, slow relaxed sexual experiences are more deeply nourishing and healthful than fast, hard fucking over a short time with a quick ejaculation. Vigorous sex can be wonderful and nourishing but it needs to be balanced with longer, slower sexual experiences.

Calm, strong, nurturing energy is so powerful. When we get to be in a 100% receptive mode we can release a lot of stored emotion.

CHAPTER 6:
Community and Conscious Sensuality

From Political Activist to Cultural Activist

I grew up fascinated by the political system. I used to live in Washington D.C. and read history books and two newspapers a day. I felt drawn to participate in current politics, working as a 20 year old in the campaign of a local car dealer who was elected to a statewide office. At the same time I was wearing a suit and tie and driving the candidate around the state, I was in my youthful admiration of the lost hippie years of the 1960's.

My idealism and political ambition were soon in conflict: When I represented the cadidates anti-capital punishment platform position in a debate with a local state senator he was campaigning against, I was told he had switched positions, even though I knew, or thought I knew his personal feelings against state-ordered murder. At that time, one could hardly be elected to statewide office in Virginia opposing capital punishment.

Another major blow to my idealism was when the first Iraq war started in 1991. After graduating from University of Virginia, I moved to Berkeley to experience a more progressive culture – whatever was left of my idealized "hippie" San Francisco – and to be far enough from home to grow my hair and become my own person. When the war started against Iraq I remember crying and pleading with my father to resign in protest. My father was a top lawyer with the Pentagon.

He had been there several years before when Oliver North and his gang had illegally sold weapons to Iran and used the money to fund the Contras in Nicaragua. I remember watching the television and seeing my dad sitting behind Colin Powell during Powell's testimony to Congress about the scandal.

I felt terribly disappointed that my dad would not leave his job and protest what I felt was an unjust war of blood for oil. I remember the shouts of "No Blood for Oil" in the streets of San Francisco where riot-clad policemen with taped-over badge numbers brutally assaulted unarmed protestors.

Reasoning the war was being fought for oil and due to the high level of consumption in the United States, I saw a connection between issues of the environment and issues of war and peace. Thus, I went back to Washington D.C. to use the tools from growing up in DC, my degree in politics and my righteous anger to pursue a career in political environmentalism.

I had dreams of running for office myself. Inspired by fallen heroes like Robert F. Kennedy, who had lived with his family in my hometown of McLean, I saw myself as a noble fighter for justice. I worked in the environmental field, winning some battles, losing some, and becoming more and more despairing of the world's environment and the possibilities for political change in the United States.

After the 2004 presidential election I was completely disheartened . I left my career and my wife, giving up my commitment to marriage and my hope for political change.

I had put my dream of living in an intentional community on hold for years due to my wife's resistance. Once separated, I could pursue my dream and create a community with the people I met that summer at the Network for a New Culture (NFNC.org) summer camps in Oregon and Pennsylvania.

Here I began my transition from environmental activist to cultural evolutionary. I began to see a link between emotions, relationships and sexuality with the environment. Just as I reasoned the war was fought to feed a petroleum addiction, now I saw how fear of intimacy, sex-negative conditioning and lack of communication skills made community living difficult. To be more sustainable we need to live more closely together and more cooperatively. Everyone living alone, or with just a nuclear family; living isolated lives dependent on cars to meet economic and social needs while being divorced from the land contributes to the environmental destruction and political impotency.

Once I joined these cultural evolutionaries I left my political career behind. How could I ever be elected to office if I went to gatherings where people espoused polyamory and had group sex?

Many of the people I met in Hawai'i were done with trying affect change in the United States and moved to Hawai'i to create the culture they wanted. They saw the political situation as hopeless and put their effort in creating a sustainable island and culture that would serve humanity after the United States, the world economy and the climate collapsed.

Living in Hawai'i has been an opportunity to build on the history of Hawai'ian sustainable ecological systems and create a culture which intentional communities are commonplace and practically mainstream.

Sense of Community

My sense of community has vastly changed since I started living in intentional communities. In the beginning it was important to me to discuss and resolve issues much like I learned from my family at the dinner table and develop or even force agreement on issues. The more I've grown into my own person, the less I need others agreement to validate my choices.

I still very much value community and cooperation, but I am less focused on creating a permanent community that will meet all my needs. When I left my wife I realized that no one person could meet all of my needs. Then I tried substituting community for wife and then realized that no one group of people could meet all my needs. I needed to meet them myself.

In Hawai'I, I feel more sense of community than anywhere else I have lived. Throughout the country, intentional communities are radically different depending on lifestyle, values, language, landscape, appearance and the community of people in the area around them. In our area of Hawai'i, the Puna District, many intentional communities thrive in addition to many people who have lived in intentional communities at one point in their life.

So there is not a big separation between the intentional communities and the community at large. This enables us to find our relationships for love, friendship, business and other interests, and not be limited to those within the walls of our house or neighborhood and/or workplace.

I imagine as time goes by that more and more people will come to see the value of living in some type of intentional community, which has shared land, consciously adopted and co-created vision and values, and an opportunity for greater cooperation and connection. Hopefully, people will be coming into these communities because they better aide them in meeting their needs, rather than just unconsciously reacting *against* what is missing in their lives.

Collectivist and Communitarian Groups

My friend and author Kelly Bryson talks about the difference between communitarian and collectivist groups. In communitarian groups, the community is valued for its role in support the growth and life of individuals. For collectivist groups, the collective is seen as the goal, and individuals subsume their growth and health for the community's sake. While no community fits neatly into one category or the other, it is useful to remember we are all at choice and that we can choose to create and participate in groups that resonate with our values and are joyful for us. Kelly likes to say, "It takes a community to raise a relationship," indicating the importance of having others witness, reflect and support our relationships.

Reflecting on the difference between communitarian and collectivist approaches, I am aware of my sensitivity to efforts at manipulation in a group context. One of my former communal living experiences had no explicit structure regarding decision-making, which led to conflict and drama. This may have been intentional on the part of the leaders or not. In any case, it was clear the leader was in charge and people either accepted her dominance or they left the community.

One of the things I remember most from this community's meetings was when the leader's partner would invariably stand up and say, "ok, who's with us?" in an effort to end a conversation and get support. And people would stand up. This kind of ploy was frustrating to me because it played on people's desire to be connected and fear of abandonment. It did not encourage people to think for themselves but to repress themselves out of a desire for connection.

This is a problem in all authoritarian structures, whether a nuclear-armed nation, a corporation, or even a small community with a defined leader: People in authoritarian groups are distracted by the power structure from discovering their desires. People either identify with the leader or the group and mindlessly join the herd, or they reject the leader and unconsciously react against the group, which defines them in terms of what they are against rather than what they are for.

Masculine and Feminine Aspects of Leadership

What is required for effective, efficient, and ethical decision-making and action in relationships, groups and communities?

Honesty. Set up systems that support individuals' connection to the truth of their experiences, thoughts, emotions and perceptions while creating rituals for sharing truth that create more love, understanding and trust. Most people have had the experience of being told we should speak the truth but have been punished for it. When we can freely speak our truth we are also freed from it and can allow our views and opinions to evolve and shift over time. If our desires are not expressed they are likely to stagnate or to come out sideways. An example of this could be if someone doesn't get their way on an issue or feel heard, they are likely to sabotage this project or some other project to prove their point.

A balance of time and efficiency. While we all may aspire to relax into a timeless space of consciousness the reality is we do have limited time in our lives and if we want to do things we need to make decisions, stop talking about it, and do it. If we do our homework and clear our emotional bodies we can step into the present moment with love and make decisions that reflect this. Often, consensus decision-making devolves into a contest where the individual with the most tolerance for boredom and bullshit wins.

Self-reflection and Feedback. Unless the feminine quality of self-reflection is balanced by the masculine quality of giving feedback in individuals and in groups we can be sidetracked by individuals unprocessed emotions. You can think of it in a gardening analogy: The feminine nurture qualities are watering, fertilizing while the masculine qualities are weeding and pruning. Are you open to pruning and being pruned?

The four primary aspects of leadership are: *modeling, facilitation, inspiration and direction.* The first two, facilitation and modeling are essentially feminine qualities while the latter two, inspiration and direction are masculine qualities. Effective group decision-making and a healthy, conscious community requires all four and a powerful, effective and ethical leader embodies all of these aspects.

Modeling: Modeling is teaching and leading through our being, our consciousness, our deeds. This is the teaching of someone who talks little but leads by example. Instead of talking about the need to develop a recycling system, this person recycles everything they can. Instead of talking about setting up a system to weed the garden they silently weed the garden without being asked or asking others to help. Modeling is extremely powerful especially if it is done with purity of heart and ease in being. It is magnetic and creates a field of resonance that encourages others to take responsibility and seek opportunities to be helpful, productive and supportive. Ghandi was a powerful model as he lived his values of ahimsa through his actions and his lifestyle not just his words. Modeling can be summed up by the dictum: Don't just talk about it, be it and do it.

Facilitation: Facilitation is the act of drawing out the wisdom, passion, and service of others. Facilitation is the feminine receptive power that intentionally creates a conscious vacuum so as to draw out the wisdom of others. In meetings and gatherings, facilitation is led by someone who is more concerned with keeping the group in a state of ease, love, trust and understanding as well as creating good decisions for everyone than advocating a specific idea, proposal and course of action. If someone has a strong agenda or their emotional field is activated or disturbed they are unlikely to be able to provide facilitation. Facilitation requires we direct our focus to others and if we are consumed with our desires and fears we are unable to facilitate. A good facilitator will serve as a powerful model when they willingly hand the role of facilitation off if they are triggered emotionally or have a desire to initiate or direct a project or agenda item. A good facilitator is not just open, but solicits feedback, drawing in other's perceptions of them.

Direction: Direction is the ability to provide guidance in what to do and how to do it. This quality is absolutely essential yet almost universally misunderstood, misapplied and feared. Direction is telling other people what to do and how to do it. It is not asking someone how they feel about their job, it is telling them how to do better. For direction to be effectively received, the recipient of direction must desire to be penetrated by the power, knowledge and experience of the masculine director. They must trust the director at least in regard to the task at hand. To do this, we must be in a field of agreement, a circle of consent and direction must be subject to review and feedback. The unconscious, abusive form of direction is where people become afraid, in reaction and become opposed to all leadership and the concept of leaders. Direction is good. Direction instructs and teaches with consciousness. Direction is when we show someone how to plant a tree, build a structure or wire a solar system. If our egos are wounded and we are unable to receive direction we miss many opportunities for growth and knowledge. Some people have more knowledge and skill in some areas than others. Obviously they should be in the directing mode of others who have less skill, experience and knowledge. Yet when we are in fear of abuse of this masculine power, we shrink from direction and create confusion, stagnancy and power struggles. Where directive power is honored there is order, harmony, purpose and profit.

Inspiration: Inspiration is the soulful poetry of leadership. When we provide inspiration we give energy and enthusiasm to others. The poet and the preacher serve as inspirational guides, using their words and their energy to motivate others. The shadow aspect of inspiration is charisma without consciousness and manipulation without consent Just as direction that is not within a facilitated process is likely to steamroll opposition and squander opportunities for collaboration and better ideas, inspiration without modeling results in skepticism and cynicism. Inspiration is a masculine, penetrative energy that moves you to action while modeling is a feminine, receptive power that draws the best out of you.

In communities where there is an imbalance of more feminine power stagnancy and confusion reigns. In the masculine dominant, emotions are crushed and people and nature are made to serve the unconscious ego. A community that is feminine dominant is vulnerable to an unhealthy expression of the masculine because it is so starved to be penetrated and directed that in it's confusion it chooses the wrong leaders to penetrate them, gets hurt and retreats again into fear, accusation and disempowerment. In the masculine-dominant community the feminine ideal is twisted into an model of needless suffering masquerading as spiritual superiority.

Hitler is the perfect example of inspiration and direction run amok in service of the masculine. While mesmerizing and brilliant in ability to control and manipulate he of course was in service to a loathsome and ridiculous ideology that was based on his unconscious psychological and emotional material. On the other side, intentional communities that reject all hierarchies and power inequalities and focus most of their attention on the emotional needs of the members would benefit from more masculine leadership.

The Role of Community in Supporting Erotic Relationships

Once, after a tantra workshop I attended, I was soaking in the hot tub at the hosts' home. The couple had given of themselves all day, created the sacred space, welcomed guests, provided for their physical needs of food and comfort and teaching their understanding of sacred sexuality.

Just hosting a gathering of two dozen people is often enough to cause a conflict before, during or after the event. To invite friends and strangers to your home and then describe your intimate sexual relationship with explicit detail is a major outpouring for the emotional body. While they remained clothed and did not perform the sexual acts in front of us, as far as their emotional bodies were concerned they did.

After most of the guests left I was in the hot tub with one other participant when the female hostess came by the tub. We invited her in and she joined us, telling us of the conflict she and her partner were having.

A little while later, after we had bonded and were all feeling close and open, her partner came by. We invited him to join us and she asked for us to listen to their conflict and hold space for them so they could work through it.

She started and related her upset about not speaking up more during the workshop and expressed her disappointment in how much he spoke. There were more details, but for me the important point was she was in touch with her need to be seen and heard.

When he spoke I had the perception that he wanted to be seen and appreciated as well and did not want to apologize for anything. They started to argue and then she asked us for help.

I gave them my perspective that they were both in a space of needing to be seen, to be appreciated and to be nurtured as both of them had been exerting a lot of energy that day. It was further confirmation of my understanding that a conflict between two people happens when both people need something that the other is not able to give at that moment. There is an empathy deficit and no amount of blaming, shaming or arguing is going to fix it.

This is where the community can support a relationship. I focused on their needs as individuals and not trying to "solve the problem" by psychoanalyzing, taking sides or giving advice. I gave them the appreciation they were both wanting. I was able to do this freely and joyfully, and was able to give them attention and energy because I was feeling full and abundant.

This is why it is so important to have counseling relationships outside of a sexual relationship. When there is an energy deficit or empathy deficit between two lovers, we need to turn off our problem solving mind and the mind that judges, and ask for nurturing and empathy from someone who is available.

When we are in a co-dependant relationship we think we have to get all of our needs met, all of the time, from one other person. When I was first discovering Re-evaluation Counseling I felt excited because I saw the potential of being able to emotionally release with another person and not drain my relationship with my wife. She was afraid that the counseling relationships would go from intimate to sexual and that she would be exposed by me talking with others about our relationship. While it can be challenging to reveal and discuss intimate details of our lives with others, increasing the circle of intimacy within a community of loving, compassionate people can do much to support our relationships.

Non-Rational Practices: Dancing and Dreaming

As important as being sober, conscious and communicating in a straightforward, understandable manner, one of the keys to building community and intimacy with others – not just a partner – is the opportunity to experience transcendental states in a group setting. Activities that promote access to our deep desires and expression of self in the context of the community are music, dance, art, theater, play, in addition to some of the following exercises.

I love to dance. When I moved to Hawai'i I connected with the Ecstatic Dance community at Kalani Honua, a local resort. Every Sunday our "church" was a large dance floor under a greenhouse roof. We would sweat, scream, pray and release all we needed to release on that floor. Rather than a religious experience focused on discussing and adhering to a behavioral code, this was a spiritual experience focused on creating and opening to energy while moving our bodies in ways that are pleasurable. This experience empowered each person to move in the way that is most pleasurable for them; moving in ways to express and release whatever is necessary to come into the present moment so we are connected to ourselves and available to fully experience the moment, others and ourselves.

It is wonderful to be in a place where everyone is having a unique experience at the same time. Some people joyfully connect with others, some are have an inward meditative experience, some are in touch with and release some emotional pain, a couple is has a slow sultry dance and someone is playing the clown. By observing people having such varied experiences in proximate time and space, we can see that energy is moving through us. We can also see the importance of remaining unattached to who is having what experience. We are all having the experience together; I am experience others' pain, joy, amusement, peace, excitement and confusion.

Free form dance is a good preparation for a group sexual experience, very similar in fact. Group sexual experiences require a high level of empowerment and ability to expand our range of sensation and emotion. They work best when we are very cognizant of ourselves: our bodies, desires, boundaries and our fears. Free-form ecstatic dance is a great metaphor for play parties. Some people at dance connect with others in ways similar to a play party except for they are wearing at least some clothes and not having actual sex. But the playful, ecstatic energy is very similar.

When Men Do Not Dance

Men have been given the story that to be light and joyful is in opposition to their status as men, as defined by hetero-centric culture. To be light and joyful is connected with being homosexual in the minds of many men. That is why there is such an impediment to men dancing in our culture. And if men do dance, they often dance the dance of conquest, seduction and oppression. They dance in relation to women, and if no women are present they do not dance. At a tantra yoga school in Koh Phangan Thailand, the male students are forbidden to dance but sit stoically as they watch the women dance in ceremony. While this serves the intended purpose of energetic polarization, it deprives men of an opportunity to develop their own inner feminine.

I find dancing to be one of the best ways to free my body, release emotions and clear my mind. In Hawai'i, and when I am traveling, I love to go to a weekly dance that is non-verbal and encourages individual exploration. It is not a partner dance or a dance where most people are standing around just watching others. People really move in amazing and unique ways.

It has helped me to feel years younger and to connect with myself in new ways. Occasionally I dance with women, or men, but mainly I dance by myself in the company of others. Dance has helped me to free myself of my heterosexual identity and my conditioning so I can experience and express more joy.

Often I see men new to our dance move through several stages: not dancing but watching, dancing a little but without truly engaging, dancing to connect with women, and then dancing for themselves. It is a beautiful progression. I find that now when I dance with women I can really enjoy dancing with them, not just as a prelude or an advertisement for sex, but just a joyful connection in that moment. I do not desire to have sex with every woman I dance with.

Dreaming a New Culture

The practice was developed by Anthony Columbo, a multi-media artist who was in residence at the Resonance Project in Hawai'i. The Resonance Project, organized by Nassim Harriman, was mainly focused on creating a new scientific understanding of physics. The community that formed around his ideas and the work of the Resonance project was fertile ground for many who were drawn to cutting edge scientific inquiry, expanding consciousness and community living.

At the Resonance Project, Anthony developed the concept of the Dream-In with inspiration from native peoples around the world who regularly sleep, and dream together. In tribal cultures, the walls of separation between individuals is much thinner and people are able to connect psychically with each other to a much greater degree than in western, industrialized cultures. Rather than using cell phones and computers to communicate many less-industrialized peoples seem to have developed unique communication technologies. That is, they have discovered, developed and retained the ability to communicate non-verbally without reference to space or time.

Said another way, these people can join consciousnesses even from great distances apart. This has been proven both anecdotally and scientifically. Yet since most scientists and industrialized people are not conscious of their capacity for this type of communication and consciousness, and the exact physical processes responsible for the connections are not easily understandable or reducible to a materialist model, therefore, this type of communication is not often studied.

By sleeping and dreaming in a group we allow ourselves to go into a very receptive, creative state in the immediate presence of others. Even without dreaming or co-creating consciousness, the act of sleeping in a group can be deeply healing and inspiring for individuals. Almost all other mammals that are tribal in nature sleep in groups. In some tribes, they have developed such a tribal consciousness that two people or more will be have intersecting dreams concurrently. That is, they are in the same dream at the same time. Considering this, the idea of a hierarchy of waking state over dreaming state dissolves.

In the dreaming state we are powerful beyond measure, only limited by our consciousness. So when we open to our dreams we greatly increase our capacity for consciousness, which increases our ability to create in the waking state. For mammals such as whales and dolphins, of which we are close relatives, there is not such a distinction between the waking and dream states. They are always in motion, in community, and whether asleep or awake they retain consciousness and conscious control over their responses to their immediate environment.

Our linear world has sacrificed creativity and inspiration for precision, accuracy, efficiency and control. While this has allowed us to manifest many incredible things on the physical plane, it has not come with a balanced, or concurrent development of other aspects of our consciousness. Efficiency, control and hyper-rationality have diminished our access to creativity.

As part of the Dream-In we set an intention to value our creative selves, the part of us that is not focused on productivity and efficiency. In dreaming, there is limitless possibility and no limits of time or space. When we can dream it, we can be it. Without access to dreams, we are locked in a limited, sterile cage of the known.

For people to experience joy and lightness in being it is imperative that we value our creative selves and have experiences of playing with others. The dream-in is one way we can play, as adults, together.

For many adults play has been highly reduced, often to the point of non-existence. Adults watch children play. Adults may play sports but this is often more in the context of competition than creativity. Competition in sports can be just another manifestation of the rational values of efficiency and productivity.

Adults may play sexually, usually in the context of a orgasm/release focused interaction. To play and create with no goal other than joy, expansion in consciousness and creative connection helps to reverse the impact of hyper-rational thinking which, at its roots, is based in fear; fear of scarcity of time, food, resources, mates, etc. When we are assured of our needs being met we have more openness to play. Yet many people are so conditioned to be fearful that they act in accordance with conditioned behavior rather than the reality of abundance that surrounds them.

Personally, I remember having anxiety years ago at the thought of non-productive time. I was working a regular, daily job, and when Saturday morning came, if I did not have a plan for the day I often went into fear and reactivity, as if my reason for existence was challenged. I was very uncomfortable with unstructured time.

I was so focused on achieving, winning, surviving, and so wanting appreciation for my hard work, that I sacrificed my enjoyment of my reward of free time. Have you ever known people like this? They seem much happier working than anything other time.

Gather a group of people together who have a shared desire to sleep and dream in proximity to each other. Set up a space where everyone can be comfortable in a bed or a mattress on a large open floor. Set intentions to dream and to remember and record dreams. One of the most useful ways to remember dreams is to set the intention, spoken out loud, before one goes to sleep. The group can chant or sing a song that reminds us to "awake" during our sleep, to value our dreams and our visions, and to stay connected with each other.

Often people at a dream-in will go into fear of intimacy or fear of sexuality and want to sleep by themselves. By making an agreement that the sleeping space is to be non-sexual and by encouraging people to become conscious of and communicate their fears, people can often transcend their conditioning and fears of sleeping in a group setting.

By setting the intention to have a non-sexual event, but one that is highly intimate, we help to make distinct the difference between intimacy and sexuality. So many people refer to sex as "sleeping together" that when we think of sleeping together we automatically think of sex.

By having experiences like dream-ins distinct from times when we explore sexually in the context of a group, we can open more fully and become more intimate when we are not in a sexual state. And by opening more fully when we are not being sexual helps us to be more open when we are sexual.

In other words, when we free ourselves sexually we also free ourselves of sexuality. We free ourselves of our obsession with and/or fear of sexuality. As we do this, our relationships and communities develop a much firmer foundation. By having explicitly sexual group events we also give permission to have events that are explicitly non-sexual. If we ban group sexual events, we drive the sexual urge underground and make every event charged with sexuality.

Upon waking, everyone can record their dreams and is encouraged to stay in a meditative state. Then when people are awake and available they can share their dreams with each other. The process of revealing ourselves in this way is another way of practicing intimacy.

The Role of Forgiveness

To forgive is to be vulnerable; to be vulnerable to hurt. To acknowledge we are in pain and we can cause pain. That we are not perfect and that we seek love and acceptance. This makes us vulnerable as it is much easier in the short run to blame, judge and keep our hearts closed than to acknowledge the imperfection of our minds, bodies, actions and words. To forgive to let go of blaming which opens us up to being blamed. To breathe in and breathe out, to let the energy of emotion move through us, shaking us to our core, destroying all our hopes, dreams and visions for ourselves, our relationships and our world.

The first step of the Hawai'ian practice of ho'o pono pono is to forgive oneself. It is the internal judge that creates fear anger and resentment towards others. Others being a projection of our disappointment with ourselves. When we forgive ourselves we create a resonant energy field that supports other's self-forgiveness and eventually communion with others.

As long as we cling to story, to judgment, to revenge and attachment to outcomes we miss the healing energy of the ever-present now. The energy of now that is so much more powerful than any hurt, pain, wrong or loss. When we close our hearts and blame we close ourselves off from the natural energy of love that pervades all. Eventually we cannot keep out love forever, for if we do we die. Eventually the power of love and forgiveness cracks open our heart and we cry like newborn babies, breathing in deeply the breath of life and love, connected to our desire for love, for the energy and joy of the present moment.

Birthing a new community

Ultimately the concepts and practices of conscious sensuality help to integrate the personal, the interpersonal and the transpersonal. When we can move easefully in our bodies and emotions as well as swimming transparently in a sea of others, we can transcend our ego and personality while retaining our unique nature and consciousness. We shed our egos and false identities and just be. We immerse in community culture to deepen with others in find ourselves in the reflection of others. Our spirituality is one of energy and consciousness. All desires and experiences are opportunities for growth and awareness. We deepen into a state of trust that our desires will lead us to a place of greater love, compassion and freedom. We get confirmation from the universe as we are supported in our journey. We are tested and challenged to strengthen our commitment. At a certain point we can see the arch of our life and understand the beauty as the rainbow of experiences leads to a pot of gold.

We become spiritual when we drop the focus on form and matter and attune to higher vibrational states. We lose the obsession and repression with bodies and sex and just let sex happen naturally. We let go of the concepts of relationship and drop into a deep state of communion and easeful relating. We are granted a vision and an embodied experience of being completely at home in our own skin and in our lives. Acceptance is a stage in dying and the death of the ego is signified by deep acceptance of ourselves and our lives.

Our hunger for connection and community is realized not created. We do not build communities, we recognize the community we are in. We feel the inherent truth that we are enmeshed in the fabric of life. When this occurs we open deeply and allow for limitless blessings that are beyond the narrow reach of our conditioned mind.